COLLECTOR'S EDITION

Entertainment WEEKLY

THE ULTIMATE GUIDE TO

Beauty AND THE Beast

FOREWORD BY BILL CONDON

Contents

Foreword

I Dared to Remake a Classic

by Bill Condon

The beloved animated film is pretty perfect, but 26 years later, says the director today, the timeless tale still has more to say.

THE YEAR IS 1932, AND THE MOVIE IS ROUBEN Mamoulian's *Love Me Tonight*. A clock strikes 6...a woman sweeps the sidewalk...a cobbler fixes a shoe...and the city of Paris starts to wake up. Maurice Chevalier's head pops out of a turtleneck, and he sings a great Rodgers and Hart song, asking everyone he meets, "How are you?" As an opening number it has rarely been matched, and it's hard to imagine that Howard Ashman didn't have it in mind when he created *Beauty and the Beast*'s equally brilliant introductory number, "Belle," almost 60 years later.

I think a lot about *Love Me Tonight* when people ask the inevitable question: "Why?" As in, "Why remake a classic movie that is not only beloved but also pretty much perfect as it is?" There's only one reason I can think of, and it's that this Ashman-Menken musical still has more to say and more to reveal.

Beauty and the Beast arrived in 1991 and reintroduced audiences to the pleasures of the well-crafted movie-musical, after a decades-long dry spell. Ashman and Menken understood that the artificial world of an animated fantasy would allow people to accept conventions that had fallen out of fashion in the six decades since *Love Me Tonight* invented them. But even as an animated film aimed primarily at children, *Beauty and the Beast* had a darkness and complexity that allowed it to connect to people of all ages. I believe part of it always wanted to break out of its two-dimensional frame to return to its live-action roots. When I was invited by Disney to attempt such a translation, I jumped in headfirst, both thrilled and terrified by the challenge.

Original posters for the 1991 animated film and its 2017 live-action remake. The director and his star relax between takes.

So here we are at Shepperton Studios in London, 80-plus years after Mamoulian re-created Paris at Paramount in Hollywood. On our backlot an entire French village is being built, under the supervision of the brilliant production designer Sarah Greenwood. Jacqueline Durran's magnificent costumes are being sewn in the costume shop; Dave and Lou Elsey's 7-ft.-tall Beast gets his final layer of fur; and fully articulated versions of Cogsworth, Lumiere, Mrs. Potts and Chip are coming to life in the prop shop.

One entire soundstage has become choreographer Anthony Van Laast's dance studio, where he works with the cream of the West End crop to create massive ensemble numbers like "Gaston" and "Belle." In the music department Alan Menken and Tim Rice put the finishing touches on one of the three wonderful new songs they've written for the movie, while on another soundstage the legendary theatrical lighting designers Jules Fisher and Peggy Eisenhauer try to figure out how a group of 18th-century partially-human household objects might have illuminated in "Be Our Guest."

Meanwhile, a more 21st-century endeavor is underway in the office tower, as cinematographer Tobias Schliessler works with armies of previsualization artists to decide how to shoot dancing napkins and utensils that don't actually exist.

And our actors! There's Emma Watson, ping-ponging from vocal training to dance rehearsals to costume fittings to horse-riding lessons, always good-humored, always with a book in her hand. Here's Dan Stevens, learning how to walk—and dance—on stilts. And there's musical-theatre veterans Josh Gad and Luke Evans, instant friends, leaping across tabletops waving wooden sabers.

Then, a moment I'll never forget: the read through. It's the first time all the participants are together in one room, able to see what the others are up to. After a brief visual presentation, the cast reads the script. One Emma waltzes, the other Emma sings. Kevin Kline touches our hearts with Maurice's sweetness, while Ian McKellen makes clock noises as only a great Shakespearean actor can. It all ends with a soaring rendition of "Beauty and the Beast," cast and crew singing their hearts out, not a dry eye in the house.

At last it's time to shoot. When cameras finally roll on Emma Watson emerging from her fairy-tale cottage on a hot July morning, I feel the jolt of what it must have been like to be in Hollywood in the early 1930s, at the birth of a new American art form. I grew up studying and devouring that grand legacy of cinema—one that a new generation of fans and filmmakers is now rediscovering, to my great delight. I only hope that in connecting *Beauty and the Beast* to that live-action tradition, we've done right both by the animated classic we all know and love, and the new medium it now inhabits.

(Clockwise) Maurice Chevalier and Marion Byron in *Love Me Tonight* (1932). Condon confers on-set with Watson. An early table reading of the remake.

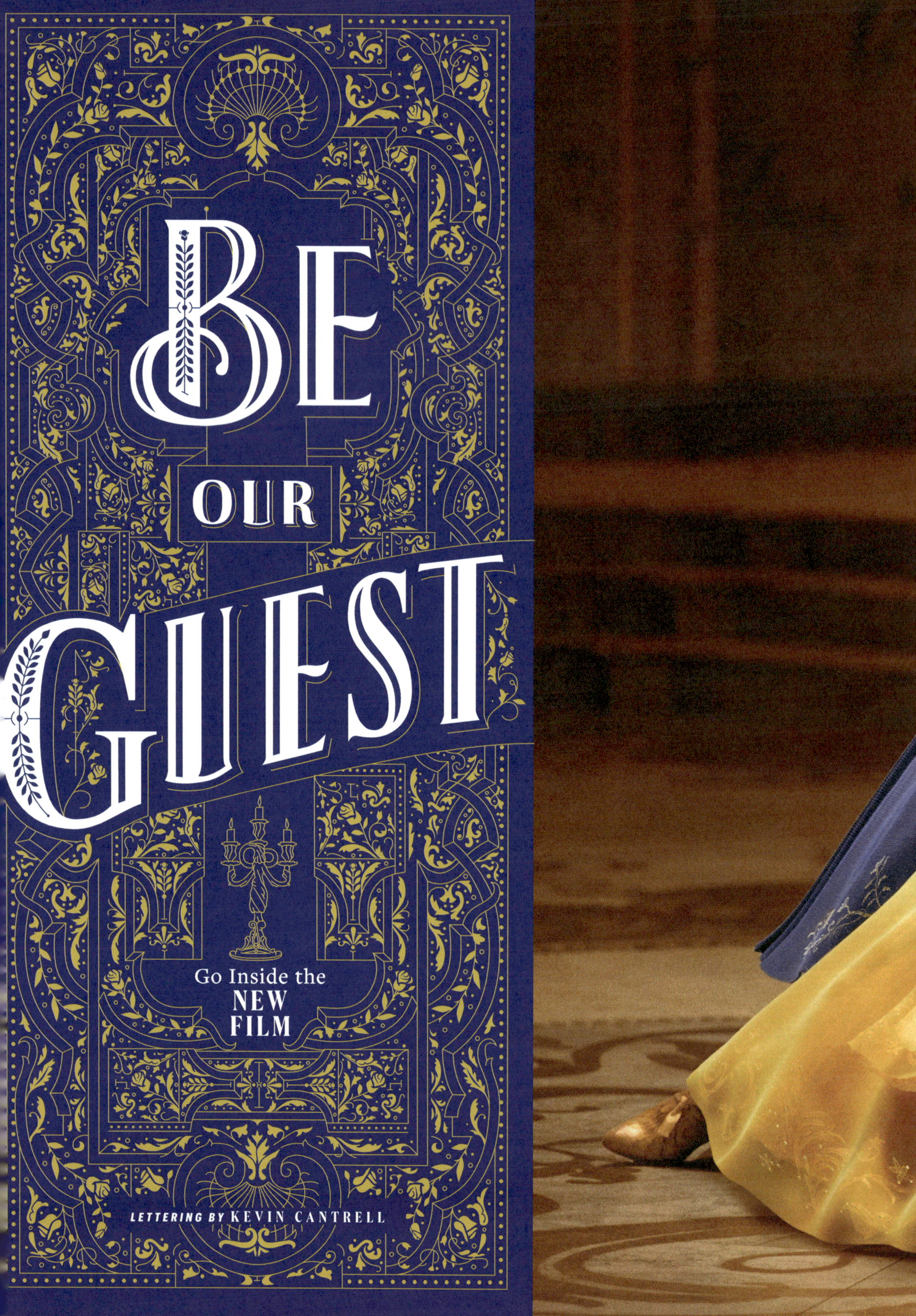

BE OUR GUEST

Go Inside the
NEW FILM

LETTERING BY KEVIN CANTRELL

Once Upon a Time... Again

Belle said she wanted something more. And now she's got it, returning to the screen in a live-action reimagining of the beloved 1991 film. Here's how Disney came back to a classic. BY CLARK COLLIS

EMMA WATSON WOULD LIKE MOVIEGOERS TO please take note of her footwear.

As Belle in Disney's live-action update of its 1991 animated classic *Beauty and the Beast*, the actress is sporting the kind of sturdy ankle boots one might choose for a long walk—or maybe a waterlogged outdoor Metallica concert. They are definitely not the flimsy flats the character originally wore as she searched for her father inside a castle belonging to an arrogant, cursed prince.

"My Belle is very practical," Watson says during a shooting break at Shepperton Studios, outside London in June 2015. "In the movie she wears these little ballet shoes, and I knew that they had to go. If you're going to ride a horse and tend your garden and fix machinery, then you need to be in proper *boots*."

That's not the only change awaiting fans who turn up for *Dreamgirls* director Bill Condon's lavish fantasy. In addition to a live cast that includes *Downton Abbey* star Dan Stevens as the Beast and Kevin Kline

Early in the process, Emma Watson helped steer her character—and costume—into more empowering territory.

as Belle's father, Maurice, there's two major new members of the castle's enchanted household staff—a harpsichord named Cadenza voiced by Stanley Tucci and a wardrobe named Madame de Garderobe played by Audra McDonald—joining candelabra Lumière (Ewan McGregor), teapot Mrs. Potts (Emma Thompson), clock Cogsworth (Ian McKellen), and others. And while every song from the original will be featured, the new film also boasts a clutch of fresh-written numbers created by lyricist Tim Rice and composer Alan Menken, the latter of whom wrote the tunes for the 1991 movie with the late Howard Ashman. These include a Stevens-performed ballad, "For Evermore," and another slow-tempo track, "Days in the Sun."

A new character. New songs. Walking boots. Put together it begins to sound like a lot of changes, but producer David Hoberman says there's no reason to worry. "It wasn't about changing anything, it was about adding dimension to it," he says. "We give [fans] everything that they expect and more—not more for more's sake, more for story's sake and characters' sake."

If he sounds like he's speaking very, very carefully, it's for good reason. Few films have inspired the kind of feverish devotion as *Beauty and the Beast*, which cast a spell over an entire generation. Topping out at $219 million in North America, it was the third-highest-grossing release of 1991 and the first animated movie to be nominated for an Academy Award for Best Picture. Though it lost the top Oscar to *The Silence of the Lambs*, it did win for Best Song ("Beauty and the Beast") and Best Score, and it went on to be adapted as a Broadway musical that ran for 13 years. But statistics and accolades can only hint at the lasting passion for the romance between the self-possessed Belle and the hirsute Beast—the cursed prince who must find true love before the final petal falls from a rose or remain in his nonhuman state forever. "I can't even think how many times I watched it as a child," Watson says. "I knew all the songs by heart."

While the new version is part of a wave

▲
Belle and her father, the tinkerer Maurice (Kevin Kline).

◀
(Far left) The Beast (Dan Stevens) with Lumière (voiced by Ewan McGregor) and Cogsworth (Ian McKellen); (left) a host of extravagantly dressed guests in the ballroom.

of live-action updates of beloved animated films (*Cinderella*, *The Jungle Book*), Hoberman and producing partner Todd Lieberman initially pitched Disney on a *Beauty and the Beast* project that presented the fable from the Beast's point of view. Following the blockbuster success of 2013's song-packed *Frozen*, however, the company instead recruited the pair for a more traditional retelling that could take advantage of the latest technology. "The opportunity to do that music with what was technically achievable—the combination of that really, really excited," says Sean Bailey, president of Walt Disney Studios Motion Picture Production.

In need of a filmmaker adept at both musicals and special effects, the producers turned to Condon, whose credits include not just *Dreamgirls* but the final two *Twilight* movies. "I saw *Beauty and the Beast* many times when it first opened in '91 and obviously saw it onstage," Condon says. "It's definitely a favorite." Watson had been attached to star in yet another *Beauty and the Beast* project, to be directed by Guillermo del Toro. When that fell apart, she happily signed on for Condon's version. "I've never sung before, but I've always wanted to," she says. Wait, she'd *never* sung before? "I sang as a 12-year-old at school," she says. "So, it was like, 'Wow, can I still do that? It's been a long time!' I did two or three months' training for this. It was nerve-racking, but now I'm in a place where I feel happy with what I've been able to do."

If finding the film's leading lady was a fairy tale, then looking for someone to star opposite her was a more grim(m) experience, in part because major stars were wary of a role that would make huge physical demands on the actor but would also ultimately be computer-generated. Condon pushed for Stevens, with whom the director had worked on 2013's *The Fifth Estate*. The actor wasn't getting his hopes up. "It felt to me like a long shot, but it was delightful when it came in," Stevens says. And not just for his sake. "For my kids as well, because they're the perfect age for this. My daughter is 7½ and my son will be

▲ Fawning Le Fou (Josh Gad) looks up to Gaston (Luke Evans).

▶ (Right) Watson's Belle strolls among the villagers; (center) Cogsworth the clock (voiced by McKellen), keeping time; (far right) Belle, with her new friend Chip the teacup (voiced by Nathan Mack).

> “We tried ... to make Belle more **PROACTIVE** and a bit more in **CHARGE OF HER OWN DESTINY**”
>
> —EMMA WATSON

5 when this comes out. They love the animated version."

And then there is the villain. Luke Evans plays Belle's egomaniacal suitor Gaston, and Josh Gad is his sidekick, Le Fou. Evans reveals that the new version gives the narcissistic Gaston, who believes he's entitled to Belle's hand in marriage, a bit of a brushup. "I'd say there's a little more humanity to the character [now]," Evans says. "He's not as brash as you remember in the film. But, you know, he's Gaston!" Filling out the household staff, Mbatha-Raw is feather duster Plumette, and newcomer Nathan Mack plays young teacup Chip.

Prior to shooting, Watson, Stevens and Condon workshopped the screenplay by Condon, Evan Spiliotopoulos and Stephen Chbosky. "I definitely had issues with the script at the beginning," says Watson. "Bill, Dan and I sat around together for a week before we started shooting and really just played the scenes out. We wanted to make sure that there were conversational moments and that they were really proper scenes, because with so much dance choreography and so much live action, it's easy to get lost in trying to make all of that work." Watson, who over the past few years has become a public promoter of gender equality and in 2014 was appointed a U.N. Women Goodwill Ambassador, was also instrumental in making changes to Belle. "We tried to tweak things to make Belle more proactive and a bit more in charge of her own destiny," she says. "In the animated movie, it's her father who is the inventor, and we actually co-opted that for Belle. We created a backstory for her, which was that she had invented a kind of washing machine, so that instead of doing laundry, she could sit and use that time to read."

For Condon, the greatest challenges involved staging the production numbers. Not surprisingly, the "Be Our Guest" sequence was especially trying. "It's interesting to do our biggest musical number with nobody there, except for some cutaways to Belle," Condon says with a laugh. "We just spent months and months and months. It's the most intricate thing I've ever worked on."

"It wasn't about **CHANGING** anything, it was about **ADDING DIMENSION** to it. We give [fans] **EVERYTHING** that they expect **AND MORE**"

—**DAVID HOBERMAN**, *producer*

▲
The monstrous master of the castle shows bookish Belle his library.

◀
Lumière hangs tight.

Stevens, meanwhile, essentially performed the role of the Beast twice. First, he acted out his character's physical movements on-set, using stilts to enhance his height and wearing a bodysuit with tracking markers to help facilitate a CG rendering of the Beast's torso and limbs. Later, Stevens replayed scenes seated in front of a bank of cameras, his features covered in ultraviolet makeup. That footage was used to create the Beast's face. "Essentially you go from these incredibly lavish sets—these amazing, tangible sets—and there's me looking like a crash-test hippo on stilts," the actor says. "And then you're transported out of there, and you've got to do all that again, but you're now essentially in *Tron*, wearing a black T-shirt in a sort-of UV booth with 27 cameras."

Ewan McGregor played Lumière twice too, in a way, first recording a guide vocal in London with which Watson and Stevens could interact on-set. He then voiced the French-accented candelabra for a second time once the shoot was over. "My French sounded a bit Spanish to begin with," McGregor says. "Then I went over to New York, where Bill Condon was doing all his postproduction, and I recorded the whole part again. I'd done a bit more work on the accent, and I got to rerecord 'Be Our Guest.'" Though Ian McKellen had worked with Condon twice before, he'd never done a musical, ever. "It was a world I knew nothing about, really: singing and dancing and playing an animated character," he says. Jumping into this world, he adds, was "a thoroughly enjoyable enterprise."

While Condon was finishing up the visual effects, Menken got to see a cut of *Beauty* and was impressed. "I was kind of overwhelmed—very emotional," he says. "It sounded great. It looked great. I'm excited for the rest of the world to be seeing it." Sounds like fans could be in store for a fairy-tale ending—and then some. "We have an amazing scene where Mrs. Potts is driving a four-wheeler through a tall building in Dubai," Gad deadpans. "We're going to give *Fast & Furious* a run for its money."

▲ Belle enjoys a good meal and a good read.

◀ Gaston and Le Fou carouse in the town tavern.

FILMING "BE OUR GUEST"

DANCE, FORK, DANCE!

What does it take to pull off a live-action "Be Our Guest," the elaborate musical sequence featuring cutlery and dishes? A choreographer, a tech team and lots and lots of patience.

—BY DEVAN COGGAN

The original 1991 animated film is packed with memorable songs, from the swaggering "Gaston" to Angela Lansbury's loving rendition of the title track. But it's "Be Our Guest" that deserves classification as the showstopper. In a film tinged with romance and heartbreak, Lumière's hospitable welcome is a moment of pure joy, as flatware and cutlery waltz around the Beast's dining room. When it came time to devise a live-action version of that culinary cabaret, director Bill Condon wanted to spare no expense.

"It's a four-minute number that cost more than *Mr. Holmes*'s entire budget," the director says, referring to his 2015 film about the retired Sherlock. "It's taken over a year to put it together—and obviously, six months before that to plan it. I would guess that it is pretty far up there in terms of the most intricate and elaborate musical numbers ever shot."

Condon says he's particularly proud of the sequence, and when he and visual effects producer Steve Gaub explain just how much work went into it, you can see why. Months before anyone even picked up a knife or fork, Condon recruited choreographer Anthony Van Laast to plot out the scene. "I'd seen a hundred animation films before, but I'd never really thought that some choreographer had put it all together," Van Laast says. The collaborators looked to masters like Bob Fosse and Busby Berkeley, drawing particular inspiration from Esther Williams extravaganzas with scads of performers. "They approached it as though they were going to put on a stage number on a Broadway stage," Gaub says. "If you couldn't imagine it [like that], then we weren't doing it quite right, you know?"

The filmmakers then recorded footage of human dancers as a reference point for the visual effects team. This took a little bit of imagination. "You'd give an animator a four-limbed dancer and say, 'Okay, now make that knife do that,'" Gaub says, laughing. Once the sequence was completely plotted out and edited, it was time to shoot real plates, silverware and models of Lumière and Cogsworth on-set, all so the camera could capture the exact lighting of each object, right down to the textures of the tablecloth or the shine of the ceramic. "I think many people are probably expecting that when we get to 'Be Our Guest,' it's going to be 100 percent CG and go for the ride," Gaub adds. "But I would say over 90 percent of what an audience is going to see on the screen started with a plate that was actually shot in the dining room set that we built."

As for the scene's only human participant? Let's just say Emma Watson wasn't sad when they wrapped. "'Be Our Guest' looks like the most fun scene to be part of as Belle but, paradoxically, was the most boring scene to be part of as Belle," she says, laughing.

▲ Belle puzzles over the mystery of the ever-wilting rose. (Above right) Gaston shows off his swordsmanship to the pub hoi polloi.

▶ Belle (right) gallops through the night and (far right) enjoys the company of Mrs. Potts (voiced by Emma Thompson).

"I'd say there's a little more **HUMANITY** to the character now. He's **NOT AS BRASH** as you remember in the film. But, you know, **HE'S GASTON!**"

—LUKE EVANS

Inside the Magic

The film's stars and creators share memories of shooting in a French village on a stage outside London. —BY SHIR LEY LI

FOR TEAM *BEAUTY AND THE BEAST*, THE movie's elaborate sets and sumptuous costumes proved to be quite a bit more inspiring than your usual day at the office. "You can't slight Disney when it comes to production values," says Kevin Kline. "It was extraordinary—one set after another, whether it was the castle or the village. It was all there."

That delight started even before filming began. At the cast's first read-through, director Bill Condon had the actors take advantage of an actual stage in the room, where Luke Evans performed "Gaston" with 20 dancers, Emma Watson sang and danced as Belle, and the team even practiced the wolf fight. "I promise you, in the history of film, no one has done a read-through like this," says producer David Hoberman. "It was almost like a full-on theater production of what the movie would be." Condon wanted the cast, which had so few group scenes, to unite and bond. "It was important because it's a movie where nobody really does get together, so it was our one chance for everybody to see what everybody else was up to," he explains. "You could feel the shift in everything once that happened."

That feeling carried over to filming at Shepperton Studios outside London, where the filmmakers and performers finally stepped onto the lavish sets, which Ewan McGregor particularly enjoyed. "We had a really lovely time of it," he says. "The actor banter [on breaks] was as much fun as what we were doing in front of the camera. It was a proper, old-fashioned British studio feeling." All of it certainly helped Watson feel as if she had been "transported to another world," one that will likely transport audiences as well.

BEAUTY AND HER BOOKS

Before production began, Watson worked closely with Condon and Dan Stevens to polish the script, adding what she calls "detail and depth and fullness and wholeness to the scenes." She also focused on fine-tuning Belle's character, expanding beyond what little was established in the 1991 film. Says Watson: "There was never very much information or detail at the beginning of the story as to why Belle didn't fit in, other than she liked books." Lots and lots of books, like the ones she's holding here as she takes direction from Condon in the library. Later in the movie we also learn where Belle and her father lived before moving to the "little town full of little people." It's a city that holds special meaning for Watson. "I sing a song called 'Paris of My Childhood,' which was odd for me to sing because I was born in Paris and my childhood was in Paris," she says. "It's a sweet melody, a really lovely song."

INTO THE WOODS

Kevin Kline's wayward Maurice, Belle's father, finds himself lost in the woods near the Beast's castle on his way to sell his music boxes at the market. If he looks safe here, he won't be for long. "I spent so much time getting pushed around," Kline says with a laugh. "I noticed it after a couple of weeks, and I said to Bill, 'I'm on the floor again.' [Maurice] is sort of the fall guy, so I get roughed up a lot!" As fans of the fairy tale will remember, Belle's papa eventually reaches the Beast's castle, a majestic but creepy estate Kline describes as "disquieting" to see in person. "It wouldn't be my first choice if I weren't stuck in a snowstorm and being pursued by these ravenous wolves," he quips. Production designer Sarah Greenwood says she and her team emphasized the castle's magic and grandeur in the grounds and exteriors nearby: "The whole landscape became part of the enchantment."

LITTLE TOWN, IT'S A QUIET VILLAGE

For the "poor provincial town" that Belle longs to escape, the crew built a real French village on the Shepperton back lot, providing a dramatic contrast between this cozy setting and the imposing castle nearby. Greenwood says her team combed French towns looking for a place to shoot, and though they found candidates in Conques and near Paris, when it came time to discuss bringing cast and crew to these actual villages, they realized it would be easier to create one from scratch. "As much as I thought it should be real, how could you say, 'No, I don't want to build a French village on the back lot'? So we built it," Greenwood explains. "That was great because we could then hybrid all the things we'd seen and put all the best elements into our village." Including a wandering French rooster. *Cocorico!*

LE FOU GETS A BOO-BOO

Filming *Beauty and the Beast* can be, well, a beast—at least for Luke Evans and Josh Gad, whose extra-macho Gaston and less-than-macho Le Fou shared bombastic scenes that sometimes led to mildly painful accidents. "We slapped hands so hard, [Josh] burst a blood vessel in his thumb," Evans (above right, with Gad and Hoberman) recalls, laughing. "We had to stop rehearsals, get the medic in. He thought his finger was going to drop off, but I think he'll survive. We just slapped hands hard, but obviously we just caught our thumbs at some point, and he's a delicate flower." But if they're sounding too similar to their characters here, don't worry: At least Gad can confirm that his hair in the film is completely fake. "If I had hair this good, I would not be doing *Beauty and the Beast* right now," he deadpans. "I would be modeling."

THE BALL'S IN THEIR COURT

It's easy to become blasé when you're an actor used to working on lavish productions. But the *Beauty and the Beast* cast never tired of their surroundings. "I remember the first time Emma Thompson and I saw the ballroom set and our jaws dropped because it's just so gorgeous," says Gugu Mbatha-Raw, who plays Plumette. The majestic ballroom (seen here) was the perfect setting for the final number, when the Beast and all the household objects return to their human form. "Just breathing it in, from the costumes to the flowers to the music, and everybody dancing and swirling around in unison, there was a real magic to it." The room also evolves with the story. "In the prologue, before he gets transformed into the Beast, it's almost as opulent as Versailles," set decorator Katie Spencer says. "Then it's an echo of what happens to him, and then it comes back for the big celebration at the end."

SINGING PRAISES

In this scene, Audra McDonald's Madame de Garderobe sings for the prince just before he's transformed into a hairy horned creature. De Garderobe craves attention, but McDonald herself responded a bit more modestly when she learned she'd won the role. "I was just shocked I was asked to be involved, to the point that when I was flying over there, I was like, 'Do they really want me to play her?'" she says. "I was pretty much in disbelief until they put the costume on me and shoved me out on-set." Which then just made her even more speechless, of course. "When I walked on-set, it felt like I was walking into a dream." Stanley Tucci (near right, with McDonald and Condon), who plays de Garderobe's maestro and husband, Cadenza, was also humbled by the splendor. "The scope of the set was enormous. They had these candelabras, these chandeliers coming from the ceiling with real candles. It was just stunning," he says.

BOSOM BUDDIES BACK TOGETHER

Sir Ian McKellen couldn't wait to slip on that wig and mustache, especially since it meant working with a director he knows well. "I've done two films now with Bill Condon, and we're always looking for a third," the actor says. "It was absolutely typical of Bill that he wanted to have a few friends with him, so I was very, very thrilled to suddenly be in my first Disney movie." Though most of McKellen's work involved voicing his character Cogsworth, the actor says his favorite moment was finally meeting the cast in person for the final celebration. "There was one absolutely glorious day when I went out and joined all the actors in doing the final scene, when all the characters in the castle come back to life and become real people," he says. "So I did feel I was in the thick of it for at least a day, and singing and dancing was an absolute joy."

PHOTOGRAPHS BY KERRY HALLIHAN

A New Slant on Belle

Upon landing the film's coveted lead role, Emma Watson let her inner child freak out. Then she swiftly got to work shaping the character to be a worthy inspiration for young women.

BY ANTHONY BREZNICAN

EMMA WATSON IS NOW 26 YEARS OLD, BUT the chance to play one of her childhood heroes instantly subtracted about two decades of poise and professionalism: When the veteran of eight *Harry Potter* films announced in 2015 that she was taking on the role of Belle in a new live-action version of *Beauty and the Beast,* she wrote on Facebook, "My 6-year-old self is on the ceiling—heart bursting."

Fairly quickly she had to drop back down to earth for singing lessons, equestrian training and dance classes. But now that the movie, costarring Dan Stevens (*Downton Abbey*) as the cursed Prince, is hitting theaters, Watson talks about her new take on the bookish, big-hearted girl who sings "there must be more than this provincial life."

Looking back, what do you wish you had known when you first learned you'd be playing Belle?

That it was all going to be okay. There were so many new things that I was taking on. I had never done a musical before. I had never sung in front of anyone professionally before! I kind of went into Belle boot camp for three months before we started

shooting, which was like singing four times a week, dancing five times a week, horse-riding three times a week.

You didn't sound intimidated, though. You sounded jubilant about playing her.
I feel so blessed to have already played one of my childhood heroes—which was Hermione—and then to get to play another one; I feel like that's unique.

What was it that you didn't want to change about her? What needed to stay the same in both the animated and live-action versions?
What I love about Belle is she is kind of the rogue. She takes a different course, and that was always what I loved about her. "I know everyone around me can't understand why I don't want what everyone else thinks that I should want, but I really just want something more, I want something else." She's like the Robert Frost poem: She takes the road less traveled.

And what did you want to change? What did you want to bring to the character to make her your own?
In the original you don't get much of a sense of who Belle is—what does she do, where does she come from, how does she spend her time before she goes and meets Beast? So I wanted to create more of a backstory for her. You get a sense of why she doesn't fit in—that she likes to read books, and she's not desperately in love with Gaston—but why is it that she's such an outsider? Why does she feel like she doesn't fit? I really wanted to get to the bottom of that.

She's revealed to be more than a bookworm—she puts her knowledge to practice as a kind of engineer, yes?
We made her this mad, wacky inventor, which was originally her father's role. Kevin Kline [plays] the character [as a] slightly frightened, nervous but very sensible, wise and loving father. So it was really fun to do that and add that on.

In the animated film the villagers dismissed him as "Crazy old Maurice...."
[*Laughs*] "Crazy old Maurice!" But now it's Belle. She essentially creates a prototype for the first washing machine.... She doesn't just invent this thing so she can disappear into a book [though]. She's using the spare time to teach a small girl to read. And the villagers smash her machine. There's a more vicious anti-intellectualism in the village this time. They don't think women should read, and it goes further than that. They are deeply suspicious of intelligence, and they don't like anything that is foreign or unknown that might be beyond their realm of experience. Breaking the washing machine is symbolic of not just them breaking something she spent hours working on but them really trying to break her spirit and trying to push her and mold her into a more acceptable version of herself.

Watson worked to fully flesh out bookish Belle's "outsider" status in the story.

This isn't far from things that happen in real life now.
I think that happens a lot with women and a lot with young girls where it's like, "Oh, that's nice, but why don't we just kind of push you this way a little bit? We prefer this aspect of your personality."

Did you face that growing up? Did you have people telling you to stay a certain way, focus on certain things?
Oh my God, the amount of positive feedback I would get from looking pretty and putting on a nice dress and smiling nicely and doing all of that. The amount of affirmation and validation that [I would receive from] that was enormous, versus studying for months and reading something interesting and being passionate about something. That would barely get a side glance.

There's been some criticism of the *Beauty and the Beast* story, saying that it's like a woman in an abusive relationship. What do you say to that?
It's such a good question, and it's something I really grappled with at the beginning—the kind of Stockholm syndrome question about this story. That's where a prisoner will take on the characteristics of and fall in love with, in this sort of really strange way, the captor. Belle actively argues and disagrees with [Beast] constantly. She has none of the characteristics of someone with Stockholm syndrome because she keeps her independence; she keeps that freedom of thought. I also think there is a very intentional switch where in my mind Belle *decides* to stay. She's giving him hell. There is no sense of "I need to kill this guy with kindness."

Or that "I deserve this"?
Or any sense that she deserves this. In fact, she gives as good as she gets. He bangs on the door, she bangs back. There's this defiance that "You think I'm going to come and eat dinner with you and I'm your prisoner—absolutely not." I think that's the other beautiful thing about the love story: that they form a friendship first, and in that gap in the middle where there is this genuine sharing, the love builds out of that, which I actually think in many ways is more meaningful than a lot of love stories where it was love at first sight.

Here it's the exact opposite!
Beast and Belle begin their love story irritating each other and not liking each other very much. They build a friendship slowly, slowly, and that builds to them falling in love. They have no illusions about who the other one is. They've seen the worst of one another—and they also bring out the best.

An Enchanting Ensemble

An all-star lineup including Emma Thompson and Ewan McGregor breathe new life into the castle's objects of our affection, while Luke Evans and Josh Gad bring comic relief to the village.
—BY DEVAN COGGAN, CLARK COLLIS AND SHIRLEY LI

CADENZA
Stanley Tucci

A new addition to the castle's crew, Cadenza is a musician married to the very fortissimo Madame de Garderobe (Audra McDonald). Though Tucci takes his character into a slightly mellower key, Cadenza does love to deliver a crowd-pleasing performance just as much as his mate. "He's sort of an extreme version of an Italian maestro," Tucci says. "He's a bit dramatic and emotional, and he's madly in love with his wife." And when the spell hits, he's transformed into a fittingly expressive harpsichord, with two levels of keys forming a mouth. Tucci, though, made sure the character mostly used those keys only for speaking—the actor had jumped at the opportunity to join *Beauty and the Beast*, but on one condition: "I told [director Bill Condon], 'I would love to work with you again as long as I don't sing,'" he recalls. "I said, 'I have a perfectly good career, and I don't want to ruin it.'"

MAURICE
Kevin Kline

Belle's papa is no "crazy old Maurice" in this live-action take. "He's not the crotchety, goofy, bumbling guy from the animated film," Kline says. "Well, a little bumbling, but he's more of an artisan." In fact, he's a painter and a maker of intricate music boxes—a quirky craft that puts him at odds with his more practical neighbors. "Imagine being a sort of bohemian artist type in a little narrow-minded provincial town," Kline explains. "He is different." Good thing he has Belle in his life. Theirs is a close father-daughter relationship, which Kline found easy to create onscreen with Emma Watson. "If I were her father, I would dote like crazy, because she's so smart and so determined and strong," he says. And in a way, he did do some fatherly doting. Says Watson: "At the end of the film, he gifted me a few of his paintings that he did whilst we were on the shoot, which I was so touched by and which are now framed in my home."

LE FOU
Josh Gad

Gaston's buffoonish sidekick Le Fou may appear similar to Gad's last Disney character, but don't expect any warm hugs or goofy snowman high jinks: Le Fou is no Olaf. This chap is quite hardy, resolute in his commitment to helping Gaston defeat the Beast and win over Belle—even when things don't go their way. "I've been chased by fire, water, every natural element known to man and a household full of inanimate objects," Gad says. "Just another day at work!" *Beauty and the Beast* isn't just a wild filmmaking ride for Gad; he considers the animated feature to be the *Frozen* of his own childhood. "I remember when the movie came out in '91. I saw it probably three or four times in the theater. I remember the applause that erupted after some of the songs," he says. "I couldn't think of a more exciting opportunity than seeing these songs fully realized now in a grand spectacle like this."

GASTON
Luke Evans

As the villain of the story, Gaston craves the admiration of everyone he encounters, but even more than that, he desires Belle's heart. "He has one very clear agenda, so he's not the best of people, really," says Evans. "But he's very fun to play." Especially when the music kicks in. The actor couldn't wait to shoot "Gaston," his character's big, boisterous number, because of how connected he felt to the 1991 film. "It was my childhood," he says. "The second you hear even the first few bars of a song, you know exactly where it's from." Gaston's bold personality made the role tough to cast, though. "Finding the right people was more challenging than they thought it would be," producer David Hoberman reveals. "We must have read and sang a hundred people for Gaston." Well, you only want the best for the best, right?

COGSWORTH
Ian McKellen

The third time's the charm for Ian McKellen and director Bill Condon, who previously teamed up for *Gods and Monsters* (1998) and *Mr. Holmes* (2015). McKellen's first Disney foray sees him taking on the persona of the perpetually grumpy but kindly clock Cogsworth, who prior to his enchantment served as the castle's butler. The Cogsworth of the new movie is far more intricate than his counterpart of the 1991 animated film, but the designers kept his familiar size and shape. "He's not a great big grandfather clock," McKellen says. "He's just the sort of clock that might be on the mantelpiece. He's reduced considerably in scale [from his human form] and probably doesn't much enjoy that."

MRS. POTTS
Emma Thompson

Thompson was blown away by the detail and time that went into designing the castle staff. "You come in and you do a bit of voiceover work, and then [the CGI designers] go away for years and years," Thompson explains. "You have kids, you get divorced, you remarry. Your whole life passes in front of you. And then they come back, and you go, 'Oh my God, you guys are still alive! This is amazing!'" Thompson had an added challenge in taking on the beloved role of Mrs. Potts, made famous by Angela Lansbury, but it wasn't the first time she'd tackled an iconic Lansbury role—they've both played the baker Mrs. Lovett in *Sweeney Todd*. She was also able to ask Lansbury for advice. "I said, 'Oh God, Angela, what do I do?'" Thompson recalls. "And she said, 'Oh darling, you'll be fine. Just be real.'" Perhaps we'll next see Thompson as Jessica Fletcher?

LUMIERE
Ewan McGregor

When it came to playing the suave candlestick who supervises the Beast's castle, McGregor's biggest challenge wasn't breathing life into an inanimate object. Instead it was tackling Lumière's debonair accent. McGregor trained with an accent coach to believably sound like a French maître d'. An additional challenge: Unlike some of the other, more stationary members of the castle staff, Lumière actually has arms and legs, which meant that McGregor had to don a motion-capture suit and record some of the candlestick's movements. "It's not [my] proudest moment," McGregor says of prancing about in character. "I had to say, 'Look, I can't do it. You've got to get everyone out. Everyone that doesn't need to be in here, tell them to f--- off.'"

PLUMETTE

Gugu Mbatha-Raw

As a child, Mbatha-Raw listened to the original film's soundtrack constantly. "I had the cassette tape in my mum's car, and I would force my mum to listen to it as she would drive me to ballet or whatever," she remembers. "I knew all the words to all the songs, and we played it on a loop." Word that she'd landed a role in the live-action adaptation sent her right back to her formative years. "When my agent called me, I screamed at the phone like I was that same 7-year-old girl," she says. On-set, there was slightly less hollering. Plumette, says the actress, has "a real elegance," even if she isn't all grace and etiquette every second of the day. "She's kind of cheeky and mischievous. There was a real sense of the flirtation between her and Lumière, so we had a lot of fun with that."

MADAME DE GARDEROBE

Audra McDonald

Everything about McDonald's opera singer Madame de Garderobe is grand, from her voluminous ball gowns to her enchanted form as a wardrobe—and to her spotlight-craving personality. The star (a six-time Tony winner) had plenty of ideas about how she'd play the part, having studied at Juilliard and lived in Italy, where she observed performers in their natural habitat. "I just grabbed the largest parts of what I knew about opera singers—what is considered the typical diva," she says. "She's a woman so completely obsessed with herself." Well, not just herself. De Garderobe is also attached to Cadenza (Stanley Tucci) in an equally gigantic way. "That passion for her husband is enormous," McDonald says. "Let's put it this way: This is not a subtle character." She laughs, adding, "That subtlety is left to other characters in the movie, not mine."

Mirror, Mirror on the Wall...

...are there any self-possessed Disney heroines at all? Yes! These leading ladies have come a long way since 1937, when the ideal princess had "skin as white as snow"; passively pinned her hopes on a prince who would someday come; and trusted strangers a little too much. Moana showed us that if a young woman wants something now, she'll jump on a boat, learn to sail and go get it herself. But it's not insignificant that it's taken the better part of a century to get this far. Over time these women have evolved into readers, archers, rebels and leaders with diverse faces, bodies and dreams. Here's a look at how that transformation happened. —BY ISABELLA BIEDENHARN

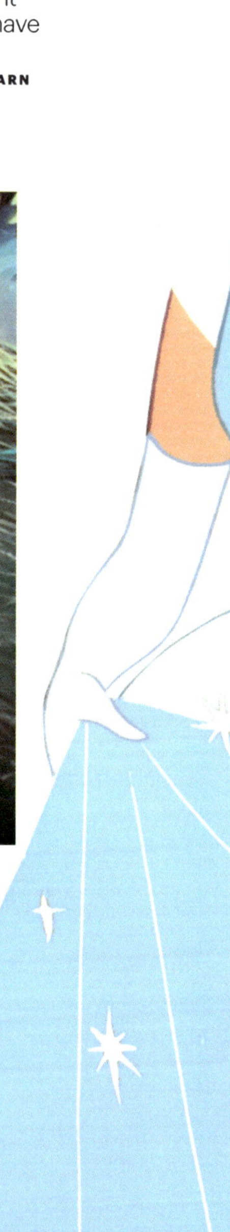

SNOW WHITE
(*Snow White and the Seven Dwarfs*, 1937)

Based on a Brothers Grimm fairy tale, Snow White led Disney's first animated feature film. Known for her beauty and kindness—much to the chagrin of her evil stepmother, the queen—Snow White befriends woodland creatures and men of small stature whose house she cleans, assuming children live there. She's a little too trusting, and a poisoned apple from the disguised queen puts her to sleep until a prince wakes her up with a kiss. Sure, it's wonderful to be nice, but are household chores and a surprise coma really worth it?

CINDERELLA
(*Cinderella*, 1950)

Several cultures have tales of a pitiful stepchild saved by a lost slipper, from China to Indonesia to Italy. Disney's telling, close to the French *Cendrillon,* brought more friendly animals, more punishing chores and more evil steprelatives to the screen. While she may be more passive than Snow White, relying on a fairy godmother's magic to get her to Prince Charming's ball, we'll give her this: Her gowns are stunning, she deserved a night out, and points for the fairy-godmother sisterhood. But in our era it's tough to watch her let her stepsisters stomp all over her without wishing she'd put up a bit of a fight. Bibbiti bobbiti... Boo.

AURORA
(Sleeping Beauty, 1959)

For a heroine who spends a good part of her movie asleep, Princess Aurora (a.k.a. Sleeping Beauty, Briar Rose) sure has a lot of aliases. Cursed by the evil Maleficent to die on her 16th birthday, Aurora is raised in the woods by three good fairies, who manipulate the curse so Aurora won't die; she'll just be doomed to sleep until true love's kiss wakes her up. Even in 1959 reviewers were bothered by the similarities between Aurora and Snow White, especially in their slumbering passivity. The only consolation is that she fell in love with Prince Phillip before she fell asleep, so there's a semblance of choice there.

ARIEL
(The Little Mermaid, 1989)

Considered the first film of the Disney Renaissance, *The Little Mermaid* pulled the studio out of its mid-'80s slump. But while Ariel's songs might stand the test of time, her story feels a little backward: She starts out as a wide-eyed, curious creature of the sea who longs to know what life would be like as a human on land. But when she trades her voice for legs (a cringe-inducing metaphor if ever there was one), she actually does meet the human prince of her dreams and eventually—voice intact once again—becomes a person herself. Achieving a dream or changing for a man?

BELLE
(Beauty and the Beast, 1991)

Belle proves that a heroine can still have that classic Disney kindness but also plenty of self-respect, along with a passion for something other than cleaning. Her looks are important to everyone around except Belle, who'd rather read her favorite book a third time and daydream about something beyond her "provincial life" than take up with the town hunk (who's a bully). And after she ends up at the Beast's castle—where he's initially very, well, beastly—he's the one who has to change for her. An improvement, even though her story still ends with romance. The original fixer-upper-boyfriend tale?

JASMINE
(*Aladdin*, 1992)

Though not the protagonist of her movie, Jasmine deserves her place in the Disney Princess Pantheon: She boasts a thirst for adventure, an aversion to empty-headed royal suitors and a shrewd awareness of her own appeal. Based on both the love interest in *The Thousand and One Nights* and Audrey Hepburn's princess-on-a-day-pass in *Roman Holiday,* Jasmine is the first nonwhite Disney princess, showing girls of all races a whole new world. It's anachronistic but pretty satisfying when Jasmine asserts, "I am not a prize to be won!"

POCAHONTAS
(*Pocahontas*, 1995)

Her Disneyfied story may not follow the facts, but Pocahontas has other lessons to teach besides history. She's a Native American woman whose respect for her people runs deep, as does her hope that peace with the British settlers is possible. She also rejects both her father's plans for her arranged tribal marriage and John Smith's offer to return with him to England. In truth the real Pocahontas married a Brit and changed her name to Rebecca Rolfe. But, you know, she also didn't have a raccoon for a friend.

MULAN
(*Mulan*, 1998)

Based on a beloved Chinese legend of a woman warrior, Mulan is a young woman who disguises herself as a man to take her elderly father's place in the army. She struggles at first but soon faces off against the Huns with brawn, brains and bravery. Even after her identity is revealed and she's discharged from the army, Mulan saves the emperor and the city. The emperor bestows on her a prestigious honor, and she gets the guy in the end—despite having caused him a bit of sexual confusion when they were army buddies.

TIANA
(*The Princess and the Frog*, 2009)

Our first African-American princess is also our first career girl: Tiana works as a waitress in New Orleans while dreaming of opening her own restaurant. When she kisses a prince disguised as a frog, she becomes one herself. They fall in love, but the time the two spend in frog form almost negates the whole diversity premise. Eventually they marry, kiss and become human again, and Tiana gets her restaurant. Congratulations?

RAPUNZEL
(*Tangled*, 2010)

Like Snow White and Cinderella, Rapunzel has roots in a classic fairy tale. But unlike her foremothers, she's a spirited, quirky character with a fully formed personality and a knack for painting. She longs to leave the tower where old Mother Gothel locked her, so she strikes a deal with a fugitive thief named Flynn to break her out. Later, Flynn is injured by Gothel, and Rapunzel nearly sacrifices her hard-won freedom for him. She doesn't—but her story still ends, like the others, with a marriage.

MERIDA
(*Brave*, 2012)

Merida, Pixar's first princess and female lead, is a skilled archer. Her parents ask that suitors demonstrate their own talent with a bow and arrow to win her hand in marriage. Merida, though, wants nothing to do with their plan. She beats them all, but her mother says her refusal to marry will cause unrest in the kingdom. Ugh—are we really forcing a 16-year-old to get married? Fortunately, the major issue in Merida's life is her relationship with her mother (and Merida's struggle to rescue her after she's turned into a bear). Her prize at the end is a happy, intact family, not a proposal.

ELSA & ANNA
(*Frozen*, 2013)

Frozen's sisters are polar opposites: The oldest, Elsa, has ice-making powers, and after an accident she is isolated in the castle and ignores her younger sister Anna, who is perky and lonely and jumps at the first prince who looks her way. He turns out to be a villain, and Anna instead falls for the unassuming good guy. Yet, similar to *Brave*, the sisters' bond is far more important than any romance; in Elsa we meet a woman with no love interest, just a boatload of internal conflict.

MOANA
(*Moana*, 2016)

Finally, with *Moana,* Disney introduced a heroine who has no marriage mandate but will nevertheless someday become chief of her Polynesian tribe. In her heart she'd rather spend her days exploring far beyond her home, but she's also quite adept at the intra-island diplomacy her future title requires. When the Ocean itself chooses Moana to complete an impossible task, she gets a demigod for a sidekick, learns how to navigate a boat using stars and wind and ends up fighting most of their battles herself, refining her sense of self and purpose.

Visual Effects Magic

Building the Beast

It's not easy being mean—or rather, looking it. To play the Prince who's transformed into a fearsome creature, Dan Stevens pulled double duty, shooting his scenes twice so the effects wizards could work wonders on him. –BY DEVAN COGGAN

THERE ARE PLENTY OF CHALLENGES THAT come with turning a 1991 animated movie into a live-action spectacular, from breathing life into a candelabra to choreographing a dance number with plates and silverware. But one aspect was a particular, um, beast. Transforming Dan Stevens into the misunderstood monster was an extremely complicated special-effects process. No wonder the actor came up with a simpler way of explaining it.

"My kids have come on-set when I'm the Prince, and it's all sort of real-ish," Stevens says. "They've also come on days when I'm doing the CGI, and I'm in this giant muscle suit with gray Lycra on. My daughter just said I looked like a hippo on stilts, which is kind of a beast, I guess. They're pretty dangerous. I told my daughter that CGI stood for Clever Gnome Imagery, and the clever gnomes take the pictures away and then turn that hippo into the Beast. And she was like, 'Oh yeah, that makes sense.'"

In reality no gnomes, clever or otherwise, were involved in the making of the hairy hero. Instead, Stevens had to play the role twice. First he'd act as the Beast, wearing stilts and the Lycra suit so animators could track his body movements (and Emma Watson would have a scene partner instead of talking to thin air). Later he'd perform the same scene again, this time with a bank of cameras pointing at his head. "Our first concern [was] well, what actor can just go back and very precisely replicate the feel of the performance that they already gave?" visual-effects producer Steve Gaub says. "And Dan gave that to us in spades." In fact, he dove into the process with gusto. "The first time they set it up, I had them play the *Tron* soundtrack because I was like, 'This is awesome,'" Stevens says, laughing.

Traditionally, animators track facial movements by placing dozens of dots on an actor's face and filling in the gaps later on a computer. But for the Beast, the visual-effects team used Digital Domain's revolutionary Direct Drive technology, where Stevens wore ultraviolet makeup that created thousands of reference points. That way the cameras could capture every twitch or muscle movement in his face.

"In my research and preparation, I had a chat with a couple of people who know this world," Stevens says. "I had a really good chat with Andy Serkis, and he was great at reminding me to just disregard the freaky stuff and to trust that all will be well." Stevens also spoke with Mark Ruffalo, who was surprised that the techniques were different from what he'd endured playing the Hulk. "He was just like, 'No, that's impossible! You can't do that!'"

With Stevens's performance locked down, the final task was finding the right mixture of man and beast. Director Bill Condon wanted the character to evoke both the 1991 animated version and the live-action creature from Jean Cocteau's 1946 film. And he'd have to be both believably ferocious and romantic. "We have to understand how Belle is falling in love with him," says Gaub, who paid special attention to the Beast's eyes, re-creating Stevens's own peepers as faithfully as possible. "If at the end of the movie, when he turns into the Prince, and you see Dan Stevens's blue eyes look at Emma, you should feel like, 'Oh, I've been looking at those eyes the entire movie,'" Gaub says.

As for the Beast's wilder tendencies, both Stevens and the animators studied how different types of animals moved. Instead of deciding on one creature as a reference point, they pulled bits and pieces from each to create something new. (No hippos, ahem.) "A little bit of very large dog, a little bit of primate, a little bit of bear," Gaub says. "But 100 percent Beast."

Additional reporting by Clark Collis

▲ Dan Stevens as the Beast in the 2017 live-action film.

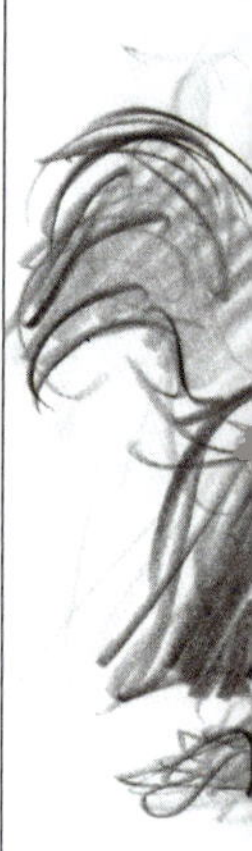

▶ Concept sketch from the 1991 animated version. (Right) One of the inspirations of the design: Jean Marais as the Beast in Jean Cocteau's *La Belle et la Bête* from 1946. (Far right) Stevens (pictured here in 2017) went blond for the role of the Prince.

"I like the **PHYSICAL** approach, engaging my **WHOLE BODY** in something. Previously it had been more **NECK-UP** kind of stuff"

—DAN STEVENS

©Disney

Alan Menken Keeps Score

Without him, some of the most celebrated Disney movies of the late 20th century—including *The Little Mermaid, Beauty and the Beast, Aladdin* and *Pocahontas*—would be, at best... less celebrated. The eight-time Oscar-winning composer spoke with us about revisiting the score for Belle and her buddies 25 years later. –BY CLARK COLLIS

What did you think when you were approached to work on this project for the third time, really?

[*Laughs*] Well, I was excited. First I heard that the studio wanted to do it, and then I had to find out, What does that mean? Who was going to direct? So when I found out that Bill Condon was directing, I was thrilled. Then it was a matter of finding out what his approach would be and what the script was. The [live-action] film version of *Beauty and the Beast* was on and off in the works for a long time. So it's been a journey to get to this point. It was both exhilarating and challenging at the same time.

When you say it was challenging, what do you mean?

Challenging because there had been a Broadway show, which had songs that I would have loved to use for the movie, but the form for a film and the form for a Broadway show are different. So the song we wrote for the Broadway show was not going to work. Consequently, we wrote a brand-new song. The challenge is just to maintain the balance of what we originally had for the score and what we had for the show, and at the same time allow this film to have its own character. So you're both the keeper of the flame and leading the way in moving on to a new vision for it.

What do you think is the appeal of the animated film?

It's probably *the* most romantic of the Disney animated musicals. It's a passionate love story and it's got a lot of depth. And in my life, of course, a lot of that power comes from the fact that it's the last complete score that Howard Ashman and I wrote together. And he never lived to see it. He was working on it as he was growing sicker and sicker, which is... the backstory to the creation of the movie is as heartbreaking as the movie is.

All of the Disney movies you've worked on are beloved. But people seem to have a special place in their hearts for *Beauty and the Beast*.

I think they have a special place for *Beauty*, I think for *Mermaid*, I think for *Aladdin*. But *Beauty* has a unique place, I think, because it was the first of any of the Disney products to come to Broadway. It was a huge Broadway show. It had that gigantic, over-the-top production number "Be Our Guest," so it's got that combination of romance and show business extravaganza.

Alan Menken (left) and his longtime collaborator, lyricist Howard Ashman, working on the *Beauty and the Beast* score in 1991. The two wrote four film scores together.

Given how passionately people feel about the movie and the Broadway musical, did you have a greater sense of responsibility than you would for something you would create from scratch?

No. Because I feel a *tremendous* sense of responsibility with something that is being created from scratch, because you're actually putting the DNA out there for the first time. In this case it's one of your children, who has been successful and now is going to be seen in another light. I feel responsible to people who love the original, but I also feel responsible—to everyone who's been involved prior to this—to be as hands-on as possible with the movie so that the flame of the original continues through. That's a responsibility I take seriously.

Do you have a favorite memory from making the 1991 movie?

It probably was the day we were at RCA Studios [in New York] and we were recording both "Be Our Guest" and "Beauty and the Beast" on the same day. We had this amazing, huge orchestra and Angela Lansbury and Jerry Orbach, two absolute classics of Broadway—I was going, "Boy, what am *I* doing here, at this place?" And Howard was there. It was not yet acknowledged that Howard was ill, but it was very clear that he was ill. So you can imagine, such a high, incredible moment, such creative power happening, and I was losing my collaborator. But it was secret. Boy, I mean, if that's not an unforgettable day, I don't know what is.

Neither Emma Watson nor Dan Stevens had much experience singing before this. How are their performances?

The results ended up being wonderful. You know, I think both of them had a lot of trepidation. They were self-protective and they were open to our input. We worked very closely with them. There was a *lot* of lead time when they learned the song, and then they worked on the song, and then we went back in and there was a lot of rewriting. It was hard work and it was so worth it.

There's clearly an insatiable appetite for *Beauty and the Beast*. What happens when the studio says they're doing a virtual-reality version and they ask you to write three more songs for it?

[*Laughs*] I can't wait for that one! That'll be great!

Singing a Different Tune

Even a faithful remake deserves some fresh surprises: Alan Menken and Tim Rice have written new songs for the film, including a ballad recorded by Céline Dion.
—BY ISABELLA BIEDENHARN AND CLARK COLLIS

LYRICS FROM *BEAUTY AND THE BEAST'S* 1991 soundtrack have been etched into audiences' minds for decades—and with the addition of 3½ brand-new songs, longtime Disney collaborators Alan Menken and Tim Rice are giving fans more new material to memorize. But...what in the world is half a new song, you ask? That would be the aria sung by Madame de Garderobe (Audra McDonald) with harpsichord accompaniment by Cadenza (Stanley Tucci) in the scene at right.

In this early sequence the Prince (Dan Stevens) is holding a ball, and a slew of young women have gathered at court in the hope of being chosen as his wife. "It's a moment within the prologue, just before the spell befalls the castle," says Menken. "The Prince is about to be turned into the Beast. He's in his very selfish and self-indulgent phase of his life, and we see that. The staff are all there before they are transformed into objects." This number, as well as the three other new ones, serve to deepen the story. As Condon puts it, "The most important thing is that a song takes you somewhere, that you're in a different place dramatically at the end of it from where you are at the beginning." Or, in the case of these poor characters, a different form.

Stanley Tucci's Cadenza accompanies wife Madame de Garderobe, played by Audra McDonald, as they perform for the Prince.

Beauty and the Beast

Vocal

How Does A Moment Last Forever

Music by Alan Menken
Lyrics by Tim Rice

1 (vln.) B♭ B♭ma9 B♭6 B♭ma7 B♭ B♭ma9 B♭6 B♭ma7
(accordion)

6 B♭ Fsus/A Gmi Dmi/F E♭ma7 B♭
How does a mo-ment last for - ev - er? How can a sto-ry nev-er die? It is

10 Cmi/F E♭/F F B♭ma9 B♭6 Gmi7 C9 F9sus F7
love we must hold on to Nev-er eas - y but we try

14 B♭ Dmi7/A Gmi7 Dmi/F E♭ma7 E♭6 Fsus/D Gmi7
Some-times our hap-pi-ness is cap-tured Some - how a time and place stand still

18 Gmi7/C Cmi7 Dmi7 Gmi7 Ami7/D D
Love lives on in - side our hearts and al - ways will

22 Gmi Gmi7 Cmi7 E♭/F D Gmi E♭mi/G♭
Min - utes turn to hours___ Days to years then gone But

26 B♭/F F/E♭ Dmi7 Gmi7 B♭sus/C F7sus F7 B♭ F/A Gmi7 F
when all else has been for - got-ten Still our song lives on___

ALAN MENKEN CHIMES IN ON THE NEW SONGS

"'**Forevermore**' is this moment where the Beast now loves Belle, and he realizes that she misses her father. He voluntarily lets her go, knowing that the spell will not be broken, but he makes that sacrifice. And as he sings this song, he's singing about how he now knows what love is. As he watches her leave, he's climbing up the turret of the castle as she recedes into the distance, just watching her go farther and farther away."

"'**Days in the Sun**' is a moment when all of the objects in the castle and Belle are going to sleep. The castle is settling in for the night, and the Beast is having memories—everybody in the castle is having memories—of what it used to be when they had their days in the sun. It's a combination of a lullaby and a remembrance of happier days."

"'**How Does a Moment Last Forever**' is done in a number of forms. The first time it's Belle's father singing as he's completing a music box, and it's 'How do you hang on to precious moments?' Then it's reprised by Belle during 'Days in the Sun,' and then one more time when she and the Beast are able to go back to where she was born. So it's a song about how you hang on to a precious moment. And then it's the song that [plays] over the end credits [sung by Céline Dion]."

IAN McKELLEN JUST WANTS TO SING!

Emma Watson, Dan Stevens and Ewan McGregor may all show off their pipes, but one cast member found himself disappointed to finally be in a Disney musical and not land a big solo number. So Ian McKellen, who plays Cogsworth the clock, took it upon himself to write his own musical showcase. "When we were in the studio, I kept singing what I thought should be a rather good addition to the score," he says, before breaking into song: "'My name is Cogsworth!/And I'm a clock! Ticktock!' But I didn't get my own song." Maybe it'll make the deluxe edition of the soundtrack?

MAN OF MANY WORDS

REMEMBERING HOWARD ASHMAN

Alan Menken reflects on his friend and collaborator, who died in 1991. In tribute, filmmakers put some of Ashman's unused *Beauty* lyrics in the remake. —BY DEVAN COGGAN

Two-time Oscar winner Ashman.

"What do they got? A lot of sand/We got a hot crustacean band!" Having won over Disney (and grateful parents) with lines—like these from *The Little Mermaid*'s "Under the Sea"—that didn't patronize kids' intelligence, Howard Ashman raised the game on cartoon soundtracks. But he was much more than a wordsmith for hire. He was part of the story team and pitched Disney on a musical version of *Aladdin*, which would include classic Ashman couplets like "Now, try your best to stay calm/Brush up your Sunday salaam" in "Prince Ali." For *Beauty*, he wrote about love and destiny, even as his health failed from complications from AIDS. "There was a huge amount of emotional conflict going on with him," says Alan Menken, who first collaborated with Ashman in 1979 on a grown-up musical based on a Kurt Vonnegut novel, and later on the dark doo-wop show *Little Shop of Horrors*, adapted as a film for which Ashman wrote the screenplay. Now the live-action *Beauty* offers a chance to hear some new Ashman gems, through previously unrecorded lines in "Gaston." Looking back Menken still sees his friend in their last full collaboration. "That was the spirit of *Beauty and the Beast*. To me, more than anything, it flows from Howard, from his heart and what he was going through."

Follow the Threads

The animated film is so well-loved that creating costumes for the live-action version required refining, not redoing. "It's really about embellishing what's in the animation rather than changing anything fundamentally," says Oscar-winning costume designer Jacqueline Durran. Here, she explains the vibrant new variations. —BY SHIRLEY LI AND CLARK COLLIS

BELLE

When it came to reimagining Belle's blue dress, "I wanted to show more to it, more than simply the blue outline of the animation," Durran says. So for that frock (and all of Belle's simple village-wear, including the red number above), she took the basic idea of animated Belle's clothing and infused it with 18th-century French period details, like delicate lacing on the bodice. The yellow ball gown, meanwhile, required hundreds of hours of work. Made of silk organza with gold leaf and glitter detailing in a pattern that matches the Beast's ballroom floor, the opulent dress was light enough for Emma Watson to move in (a lack of a corset helped). And it's not meant to be an exact replica of its hand-drawn predecessor. "I really believe that if you are a fan of the original movie, if the dress didn't in some way reinterpret that original dress, it would always be slightly disappointing," Durran says. If you look closely at Belle's accessories, they too evoke the Beast's dwelling. "There are elements that are the results of the castle being a living thing and creating this costume," the designer says, noting the plantlike cuff on Belle's ear, the feather motif repeated in the hair ornament and the organic gold filigree necklace, which Durran says "is a sort of magic reinterpretation of the tree of life."

THE BEAST

The Beast may be a (former) man of few words, but his costumes tell a rich story. Early in the film he doesn't wear much clothing at all; instead, he hides behind shredded cloth that forms a cape. "There's not anything human to him at the beginning, and then slowly human elements are reintroduced," Durran says. As he falls deeper in love with Belle, he starts caring about his wardrobe again—and the household-staff-turned-objects are eager to assist. "We thought about how the objects would have been rallying around to try and help him become the prince that Belle would fall in love with," Durran says. For example, when it came to the outfit the Beast wears to the ball (above), Durran's team imagined Plumette painting the design onto it, making the embroidery look like gold print. Not that it's easy dressing a Beast: Durran had to make garments that stretched and moved with the animal-like character, which required alternately working with the visual-effects department, a physical mold, a stuntman and actor Dan Stevens. Even the Beast's beard was a challenge. As Durran puts it, "Collars are not problems you usually deal with." Ruffly neckwear—how beastly!

MADAME DE GARDEROBE & CADENZA

The limelight-loving pair—she's a singer, he's a harpsichordist—needed costumes to match their bold personalities. So Durran looked to classic 18th-century French fashions worn by royal performers and added subtle, enchanting details to their looks which were in keeping with the garb of the other castle denizens. For the outfit Stanley Tucci wears as Cadenza, she says, "we cut up gold lace fabric and appliquéd it on the coat and waistcoat to create the impression of embroidery. It was one of my favorite things in the film's costumes." Audra McDonald's dress wasn't as delicate. As Madame de Garderobe, the actress wore a gown that reflected the interior's grandeur and evoked the stately wardrobe she becomes once the witch's spell is cast. "I really wasn't prepared for how they would have me mirror [the wardrobe] in human form," McDonald says. "She's humongously glorious, and the costume was so big I couldn't sit down in between takes."

GASTON

No one's slick like Gaston, no one's quick like Gaston—and few probably focus on their looks as Gaston. Here, the egotistical villain's signature red returns to the big screen first in costumes influenced by an 18th-century army uniform (above). Not that this poseur has ever been in the line of fire, of course. Gaston just always wants to appear as impressive as possible, hence the predominance of extravagantly embellished jackets that Luke Evans wears throughout the film. "It's all about vanity and the impression he wants to give off of pure masculinity," Durran says. "Because he's so vain, he keeps having to add details to himself. He's always kind of pumping himself up and making sure he looks the most extraordinary."

MAURICE

Just as Emma Watson gave input to Durran as they worked to craft Belle's look, Kevin Kline weighed in on the aesthetic direction of his character, Belle's papa. "Kevin had a strong feeling of [Maurice's clothing] being influenced by an artist's smock, so his smock coat was made of linen like an artist's," Durran says. "It was really about capturing the sense of an 18th-century artist and someone who's come from Paris and moved to this backwater village and how he'd stand out." And though in the new version Belle is now the inventor of the family, Maurice remains as quirky as ever. "He's absentminded, and Kevin wasn't uncertain about his interpretation," Durran says. "At one point I think he kept two pairs of glasses on. He's a lovable eccentric."

LE FOU

As much as Le Fou hopes to copy Gaston, all he can muster is a "washed-out version" of Gaston's look, Durran says. That idea manifests in the limp necktie actor Josh Gad wears—a small token connecting the meek lackey to the man he idolizes. "He can't be the full Gaston because he's nowhere near good enough, but copying him by having a red necktie counts," Durran says. "He couldn't really aspire to have any of the fashionable or military details." Still, Gad didn't have any qualms about his costume being a pale imitation of his costar's; Durran remembers the actor being delighted just to try on his outfit at his first fitting. "He did a lot of singing," she says with a laugh. "Comic, operatic singing."

Sets to Make Us Swoon

Production designer Sarah Greenwood explains how she built a gorgeous French castle straight out of a fairy tale.

BY DEVAN COGGAN

BEING THE PRODUCTION DESIGNER ON A FILM as big as *Beauty and the Beast* can be intimidating. Not only is Sarah Greenwood responsible for the look of a massive Disney project, but she has the added pressure of reimagining a fairy tale beloved by millions. Oh, and there's the small matter of designing and building an entire castle. "As a story, you think, 'Oh, that's simple. It's a village, it's a wood, it's a castle,'" Greenwood says. "It's so complicated. *So* complicated."

Greenwood and director Bill Condon wanted their take on *Beauty* to feel even more luxurious and magical than ever before. They oversaw sprawling sets packed with historically accurate details, from the chandeliers in the ballroom to the books in Belle's library. The designers used the 1991 animated film and Jean Cocteau's 1946 romance as a reference, complemented with some good old-fashioned imagination. "To design a fairy-tale castle," she says, summing up the experience. "Are you telling me that's not the biggest treat in the world?"

The Beast's snow-dusted palace at sunrise. His impressive dwelling was modeled after real French châteaus and the Cinderella castle seen on the Walt Disney Pictures logo.

HAVING A BALL

For the Beast's 12,000-sq.-ft. ballroom, Greenwood and her team went for full-on glamour and romance, adding details like 10 separate 14x7-ft. chandeliers, all modeled on those in the Hall of Mirrors at Versailles. "Once it's populated with the songs and the characters, it just completely comes to life," Greenwood says. And if you look closely, you may spot a few Easter eggs in the finished film: The faux-marble floor is inspired by the ceiling of a Benedictine abbey in Braunau, Germany, to which Greenwood added a "W.D." monogram honoring Walt Disney.

ROCOCO REDUX

Beauty and the Beast's 1740s setting places it smack in the middle of the rococo period, and the elaborate, luxurious style lent itself perfectly to the idea of an enchanted castle. "All our draft people had to do rococo boot camp," Greenwood says, laughing. "What we didn't want was something that was going to get kind of dank and overgrown. Rococo worked really well because it's so effervescent."

HOME SWEET HOME

The home that Belle shares with her father, Maurice, may be a stark contrast to the opulence of the Beast's castle, but the 18th-century detail is still there. One of the crew's biggest challenges was constructing the intricate music boxes Maurice crafts for his daughter. "She's overprotected in a way by her father because she's lost her mother," set decorator Katie Spencer says. "So we've made all these music boxes that represent different countries of the world, so she can see what she's missing."

A CASTLE FIT FOR A PRINCESS

The Beast's sweeping grounds and hedges were inspired by the elegant baroque style of France's Château de Vaux-le-Vicomte, while the actual architecture borrows heavily from the Château de Chambord and its jaw-dropping French Renaissance roof. "Unlike a lot of Disney fairy stories, this was set in France in an actual period," Greenwood says. "So although it's still fantastical, it definitely came from somewhere real."

FOUNTAIN OF INSPIRATION

Initially, Greenwood thought the film would shoot on location in real French villages like Conques and Noyers-sur-Serein, but instead the crew built a sprawling village at Shepperton Studios outside London, covering 28,787 sq. ft. Although the architectural details are primarily French, Greenwood modeled the town's fountain on a similar one in Rothenburg, Germany. "We kind of poached the best elements and put them in our village," she says. The final touch? The filmmakers named their quaint town Villeneuve, after original *Beauty and the Beast* author Gabrielle-Suzanne Barbot de Villeneuve.

A LAVISH LIBRARY

In the animated film, no setting inspires as much awe (or envy) as the massive library in the Beast's castle. To build the literary sanctuary, Greenwood took inspiration from a library in Portugal and added elaborate ceiling frescoes. "It's described in the script as the biggest library in the world, but we didn't want it to be just big," she explains. "It didn't have to feel like a place you wouldn't be allowed into. It had to have a warmth and openness about it."

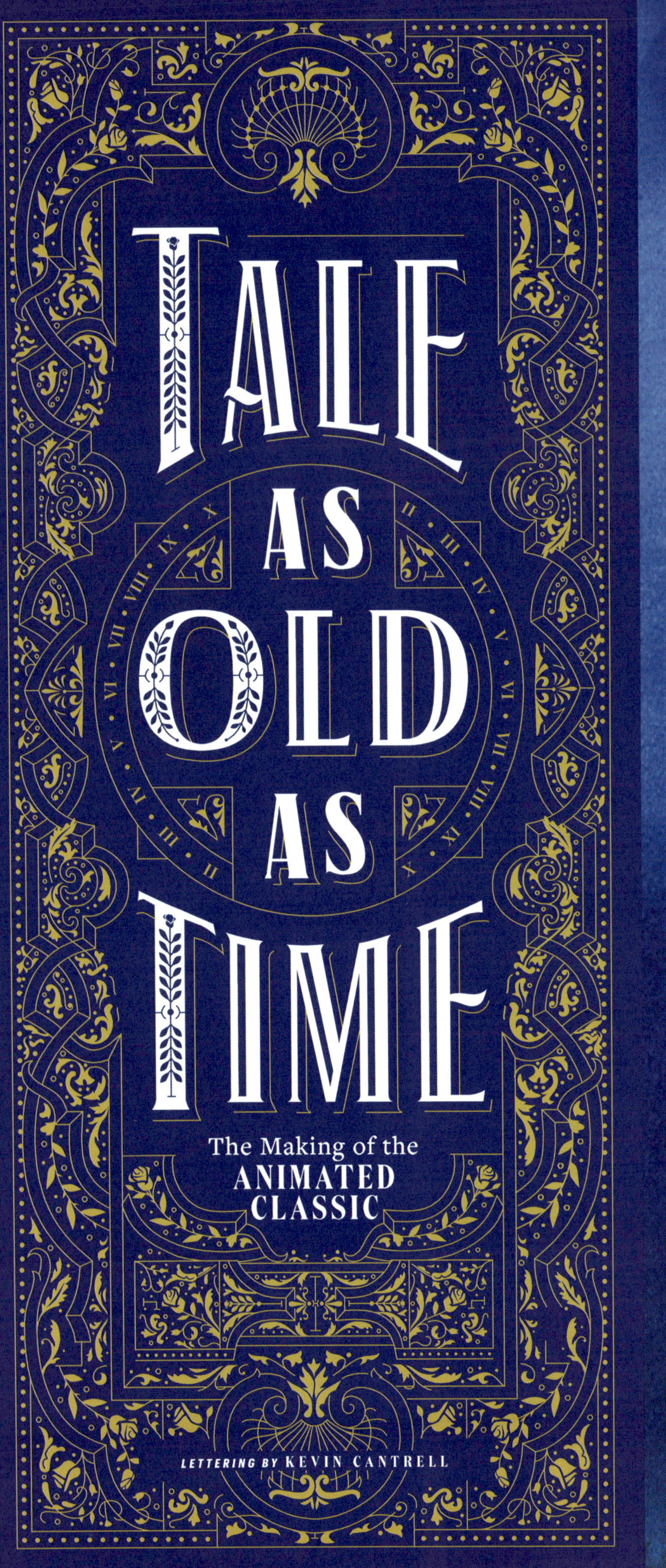

TALE
AS
OLD
AS
TIME
The Making of the
ANIMATED
CLASSIC
LETTERING BY KEVIN CANTRELL

The Evolution of the Story

It's a tale as old as...oh, you know. We trace the enduring yarn of the captive maiden and her monster-man from prehistoric days to this year's live-action movie. —BY DEVAN COGGAN

ORAL ORIGINS

In an extinct Indo-European language, our prehistoric ancestors begin sharing a folktale that anthropologists have recently reported to be among the earliest roots of the fairy tale we know today.

1537
A REAL-LIFE BEAST

A basis in (furry) facts? Petrus Gonsalvus is born in the Canary Islands, his body covered in a coat of animal-like hair—an affliction that makes him look like a wolf. He is educated at the court of Henry II in France and marries a noblewoman with whom he has six or seven children, four of whom share their father's wooly appearance. His life is said to be one inspiration for the novel that appeared 200 years later.

1740
THE NOVEL

Gabrielle-Suzanne Barbot de Villeneuve publishes *La Belle et la Bête,* the first known written version. In this telling, the cursed prince is a *bête* in both senses of the French word: He's a beast who's also dumb.

1983
STEVIE NICKS'S SONG

The singer includes "Beauty and the Beast" on her album *The Wild Heart.* Nicks has shown footage of the Cocteau movie while performing the tune in concert.

1984
KITSCHY CULT TV

Susan Sarandon and Klaus Kinski play the handsome/homely pair in an episode of Shelley Duvall's oddball TV series *Faerie Tale Theatre.* Upping the pop-culture trivia ante: This installment is directed by *Barbarella*'s Roger Vadim.

1987
THE STORY...IN SONG

The musical *Beauty and the Beast* was shot in Israel and stars *Risky Business*'s Rebecca De Mornay as the put-upon daughter of a merchant who falls for a hirsute prince (played by John Savage of *The Deer Hunter* fame).

1994
THE BROADWAY SHOW

Disney unexpectedly takes the Great White Way by storm with a stage adaptation of its animated film, which paves the way for future Mouse House adaptations including *The Lion King* and *Aladdin.*

2009
AN ATTEMPT AT HORROR

Belle (Estella Warren) and the Beast (Victor Parascos) team up to hunt a killer terrorizing a village in this schlocky rendition. Perfect if you like your stories with as much blood, camp and cleavage as possible.

2011
A TEEN-TARGETED SERIES

The classic story gets a YA update with *Beastly,* introducing star-crossed New York City high schoolers Kyle (Alex Pettyfer) and Lindy (Vanessa Hudgens). Mary-Kate Olsen is the witch who curses Kyle to a year of baldness and bad face tattoos. Way harsh.

1756
THE SHORTER NOVEL

Jeanne-Marie Le Prince de Beaumont republishes an abridged variation of de Villeneuve's narrative, eliminating much of the Beast's backstory and simplifying the plot. It's a hit, though she gives no credit to de Villeneuve. Tsk-tsk.

1946
AN EARLY MOVIE

French avant-garde artist, writer and filmmaker Jean Cocteau releases the moody, taciturn *La Belle et la Bête*, starring Josette Day and Jean Marais. Roger Ebert later called it "one of the most magical of all films."

1952
A SOVIET CARTOON

Based on the Russian story by Sergey Aksakov, the animated short *The Scarlet Flower* takes a different approach, focusing on a father of three daughters who is thrown overboard during a storm and washes up on a monster's island.

1962
AN AMERICAN FILM

The first English-language live-action screen adaptation comes from B-movie director Edward L. Cahn, whose lasting claim to fame is 1958's *It! The Terror from Beyond Space*. Mark Damon stars as the melodramatic prince who's only beastly part-time, transforming, like a werewolf, each night after the sun goes down. *Aaaaaaoooooooo*!

1987
THE MODERN-DAY TV SERIES

Belle in the Big Apple: Linda Hamilton is a Manhattan lawyer whose life is transformed when a nobleman-beast named Vincent (Ron Perlman) rescues her from an attack. The cult show, which still boasts a vocal fandom, ran for three seasons. (Fun fact: *Game of Thrones'* George R.R. Martin served as a writer.)

1991
THE CERTIFIED CLASSIC

Bonjour! Disney releases its animated musical, a box office and critical smash that makes history with a Best Picture Oscar nomination.

1993
A HOWLER OF A MUSIC VIDEO

The Michael Bay-directed clip for Meat Loaf's "I'd Do Anything for Love (But I Won't Do That)" features the musician emoting as the Beast in a haunted castle—plus a hammy scene of him running from the police and plowing his motorcycle through a wall. Badass.

2011
THE META TV HIT

The ABC series *Once upon a Time* premieres, with Belle played by Emilie de Ravin. The Beast is (spoiler!) Robert Carlyle's Rumpelstiltskin. In a later season the pair re-create the 1991 film's ballroom dance, yellow dress and all.

2012
A GOVERNMENT-CONSPIRACY TV SERIES

Loosely based on the 1987 show, the CW series *Beauty & the Beast* lasts four seasons and stars Kristin Kreuk and Jay Ryan. She's a sexy detective; he's a supersoldier who's been manipulated by a secret government organization and whose only disfigurement is a single scar on his cheek.

2014
***UN NOUVEAU* FILM**

Directed and cowritten by Christophe Gans, *La Belle et la Bête* returns to its French roots and stars Léa Seydoux and Vincent Cassel.

2017
DISNEY'S LIVE-ACTION REMAKE

Director Bill Condon tries his hand at another version, with an assist from Emma Watson and Dan Stevens as the mismatched pair.

A Beast of a Task

Walt Disney long wanted to make a cartoon *Beauty and the Beast* but didn't see it in his lifetime. Here's the story of how it came about, told by the people who brought it to life. —BY STEVE DALY

IT WAS SUMMER 1989, AND DISNEY STUDIO chief Jeffrey Katzenberg thought he might finally realize a dream that had eluded Walt Disney himself: adapting the French fairy tale "La Belle et La Bête" as an animated film. The British husband-and-wife directing team Richard and Jill Purdum would oversee development of a nonmusical version in London, collaborating with a team from Disney's animation facilities in California—producer Don Hahn (just off *Who Framed Roger Rabbit*), screenwriter Linda Woolverton (a TV-animation veteran) and a number of artists, including Glen Keane, who began developing the look of the Beast. Then the whole gang would come back to Los Angeles to begin production. Except it didn't work out that way. In September Hahn and Dick Purdum flew to Orlando, where Jeffrey Katzenberg was visiting a new ancillary animation studio the company had just built inside Walt Disney World. Hahn and Purdum privately showed Katzenberg a 20-minute reel of rough sketches and temporary vocals. There were no songs. Belle had a little sister with a cat and a mean, greedy aunt who wanted to marry her off to rich Gaston. With one exception, none of the enchanted-castle objects had faces or voices. Katzenberg was unimpressed.

ANIMATOR
GLEN KEANE
We were waiting back in London. Don [Hahn] pulled us together and said, "Well, I've got good news and bad news. The good news is, we're still going on a five-day research trip to the Loire Valley in France tomorrow to study the châteaus. The bad news is, everything you've worked on so far has been thrown out."

▲ David Ogden Stiers, Angela Lansbury and Jerry Orbach recording their characters.

► "If you look at all the gals we've created over the years, Belle is more on the mature side," says animator Mark Henn (right). "Late teens, early 20s is how I pictured her."

CODIRECTOR
KIRK WISE
[Disney execs] decided they wanted to pull Howard [Ashman] and Alan [Menken] into the mix and turn it into a musical, because the version the Purdums were working on was very straight, very dramatic. It lacked that Disney charm we all know and love. Howard suggested that the "object" characters, which were previously sort of silent pantomimes, be full-on speaking and singing characters. He proposed ideas for musical numbers. The Purdums decided this wasn't the movie they signed on to make, so they graciously bowed out. That left an empty space in the directors' chairs. But Gary and I weren't feature directors. I think they were happy with "Cranium Command," this crazy five-minute short we directed for Epcot Center. I guess they figured, Why not give these guys a shot?

CODIRECTOR
GARY TROUSDALE
Kirk and I got called in by the head of the development department. Christmas was three weeks away. He said, "Can you be on a plane in two days to New York? You might get to direct *Beauty and the Beast*." I didn't really have that great a time directing "Cranium Command." I like drawing. Directing was a lot of work—and not a lot of fun work. So I said, "Can I think about it?" And [development head] Charlie [Fink], God bless him, said, "No!" And that was that.

The new creative team now also included three gifted story artists who would go on to become directors themselves: Chris Sanders (How to Train Your Dragon), *Brenda Chapman* (Brave) *and Roger Allers* (The Lion King). *They all spent the winter of 1989-90 banging out a brighter, funnier, song-filled plot while headquartered in dowdy conference rooms at a Residence Inn in the upstate New York town of Fishkill, near Ashman's home in Beacon. Ashman, by then sick with AIDS but keeping his illness from the team, was worried he'd become too weak to travel to L.A. much during production.*

Beast concept art, 1991.

(Left to right) Menken, Ashman, conductor-vocal arranger David Friedman and orchestrator-songs arranger Danny Troob.

GARY TROUSDALE
Howard was smart. I mean really, really smart. He could form an idea, articulate it and argue it on the fly, in a way that would just leave you standing in the dust. He clearly knew the Broadway musical-theater discipline. But he liked cartoons, he liked the Beatles, he liked popular music, he liked movies, he liked campy stuff, so he was easier to talk to than some other lyricists. He wasn't a theater snob.

SCREENWRITER
LINDA WOOLVERTON
I hit it off right away with Howard, even though I didn't come from musical theater. Howard and I wanted to make a sea change in the Disney heroine. Together we conjured up Belle, who loved to read. She was unconscious about her beauty. She had dreams of faraway places, and she wasn't a victim; she's not sitting around waiting for anybody to rescue her or [for] a prince to come. We of course came into a lot of pushback about it. There was a template of what a Disney heroine should be: taking all of this abuse, smiling and talking to little animals through it all. That's not what I felt the world needed. I used to rail about it, honestly. I didn't make myself very popular. Which I'm sure you'll hear.

PRODUCER
DON HAHN
The storyboard artists weren't used to

“Gaston was gonna be this big, broad, **SWAGGERING** guy. People are most critical of human characters, so we had to push it but in a believable way”

—GARY TROUSDALE

having a screenwriter in the same room, and Linda, uh…Linda's manner at times could be combative. And I would say that if she were in the room with me right now. It was an unusual [and] difficult, tense relationship with Linda. But…Howard liked her, and Jeffrey saw that Linda would be a good collaborator with Howard.

KIRK WISE

The visual possibilities were leaping off the page with every rhyme Howard turned in. He had a great imagination and a tremendous sense of humor. But like many artists, he was also extremely passionate. And he could be very stubborn.

DON HAHN

Howard was a very intense guy. He used to chew legal pads. Like he'd rip off a piece of paper and wad it up, stick it in his cheek like chewing gum. And he'd work over these amazing couplets and rejoinders of words. He didn't suffer fools. But he wasn't a jerk. He was incredibly big-hearted. He would come in with donuts from his favorite bakery every day. Our story crew would pitch ideas, and Howard would musicalize them. Alan Menken was kind of a short-order chef, serving up melodies in the appropriate style. When the songs started coming in, it was like winning the lottery. First came the two opening numbers, "Belle" and "Belle's Reprise," on the same tape with "Be Our Guest." The title ballad came in on a separate tape a few weeks later.

COMPOSER

ALAN MENKEN

Howard was pretty apoplectic when we FedExed those cassette tapes. He was saying, "We can't send a seven-minute opening number to Disney. Nobody asked for that." But they went crazy. They loved it.

In March 1990, Ashman told Menken he had AIDS and asked him not to tell anyone else on the Beauty *crew. Menken contained his grief as best he could. Meanwhile the production team was settling the casting of the voice actors who'd play the title characters, and the artists and animators who'd draw those characters.*

KIRK WISE

[For Belle], a seemingly endless procession of Broadway leading ladies were trotted out in front of us. Gary and I would deliberately shield our eyes and just look down. We didn't want to be swayed by a particular actor's look. We wanted to see if we could hear that voice coming out of this drawn character.

PAIGE O'HARA

VOICE OF BELLE

I was living in New York, working in the theater. I read about the movie in *The New York Times* and called my agent. I know they'd been thinking about using Jodi Benson [who had voiced Ariel in *Little Mermaid*] again. Then they all decided they wanted to go for a little bit older sound for Belle—more mature, warmer—and there's a certain lower midrange to my voice. It was actually the Beast that they had the hardest time casting. I was in recordings for months, and they hadn't found him.

GARY TROUSDALE

The Beast was a real challenge. We went through Hollywood; we went through New York. So many people. We were going through story meetings and effects meetings and layout meetings, and our casting guy Albert Tavares was still doing Beast casting calls.

"Katzenberg thought if I met Robby Benson, I'd end up drawing the character like a heartthrob sort of a guy," says animator Glen Keane (above). "He actually forbade me to go to any of Robby's recording sessions."

Paige O'Hara and Robby Benson voicing the leads.

ROBBY BENSON

VOICE OF BEAST

I had been teaching at the University of South Carolina but moved back to Los Angeles with my wife, Karla, and our daughter. Right after I got back, I got a call from my agent: "There's an animated movie, and they're looking for a deep bass voice." My agent knew from working with me that my real tones are baritone to bass. So I went in to Disney in Burbank for my first audition. I'm sitting outside and I could hear other actors blowing the roof off the place with their big, growly beast voices. Really wonderful actors, but I heard them fall into a trap. They only played the Beast angry.

KIRK WISE

Albert Tavares played Gary and me a cassette, and the voice was an amazing mix of youth and vulnerability and a little bit of pain. There was gruffness, but there was humor. It was the first person to read for the role that actually could find lightness in certain scenes and bring a smile to it. So we asked, "Who is it?" "Robby Benson." We both paused and said, "Robby Benson? *Ice Castles* Robby Benson?"

DON HAHN

Robby's career was not doing well at the time. Years before, he was a teen idol and he had done *Ice Castles.* We had just cast Robin Williams in the lead [as the Genie] on *Aladdin,* and so it was odd, because [Robby] wasn't necessarily a celebrity. But he was so good we thought, We have to go with him. The studio didn't want us to talk about it at an early press preview. There was this fear that we were casting some sort of press pariah—that it would become the dominant story about the movie. It was really awkward. We didn't tell Robby.

ROBBY BENSON

Pop culture really does put you in this time capsule. And those first images of who you are to people sometimes just never go away.

Somewhat easier was the casting of the castle's comic-relief trio: veteran song-and-dance man and Law & Order *star Jerry Orbach as the Maurice Chevalier-accented candlestick Lumière;* M*A*S*H*'s David Ogden Stiers as Lumière's stuffy nemesis, Cogsworth the clock; and Angela Lansbury, still starring in* Murder She Wrote, *as the Cockney teapot Mrs. Potts.*

ALAN MENKEN

The model for Mrs. Potts was Mrs. Bridges, the cook from *Upstairs, Downstairs.* And we wrote the song "Beauty and the Beast" with Angela in mind.

ANGELA LANSBURY

VOICE OF MRS. POTTS

I was good friends with Disney because of [the 1971 fantasy musical] *Bedknobs and Broomsticks.* I always felt I was kind of a kindred spirit.... I could understand them coming back to me to consider playing Mrs. Potts. It just made me laugh, to be honest with you—the whole idea of playing a teapot who has rather an important role in the coming-together of the Beast and herself. I thought, Well, why not?

The principal voice cast recorded their songs in early 1991, but a shadow hung over the production. Howard Ashman was hospitalized at St. Vincent's in Manhattan. Though bedridden, he continued to contribute notes and turned out a final few songs for the upcoming film Aladdin.

ALAN MENKEN

There were times where it got so difficult

▲
(Above left) Concept art of the Beast's castle. (Above) Angela Lansbury with husband Peter Shaw and grandchildren at the premiere in Los Angeles.

►
Belle and her inventor father, Maurice, who was voiced by Rex Everhart.

to be in the room with Howard that I would have to leave. I would literally go and just cry. The amount of pain in the room was palpable. And I was getting beaten up pretty badly. Howard was always impatient about getting what he wanted. But now it was so intense. At one point he had a problem plugging in a faulty microphone to a Walkman Pro, which now would be like a $1,500 piece of equipment. And he took the Walkman Pro and smashed it against the wall. I was in shock. I started to go over to pick it up, and he said, "Don't touch it." I think it was just Howard going through a lot of pain about his mortality.

DON HAHN
We had a press event in New York in February 1991 previewing some of the songs. The response was remarkable. Afterward a group of us went to visit Howard in his hospital room. It was me, Jeffrey Katzenberg, Peter Schneider and David Geffen. That was just a stomach punch, after such a huge reaction, to go see Howard, literally on his deathbed. He's lying in bed, thin and gaunt, without a voice. He's wearing a *Beauty and the Beast* sweatshirt that we sent him. His mom and sister were there. We said our goodbyes one at a time. It was a chance to lean over and give him a hug and try to tell him—not only what he meant to us personally but what he meant to the audience, what he meant to Broadway. I can't tell you how heartbreaking it was.

ALAN MENKEN
The morning Howard died [March 21, 1991], I had this dream that I visited him at the hospital. He was wearing a black robe. Then I jolted awake. It was 6:30. And it turned out that was when Howard died.

DON HAHN
The movie had to be finished. That was difficult. But it was also a positive reminder of Howard's contribution. To be able to turn our backs on the illness and the darkness of it all, and keep our heads down and keep working, was therapeutic for all of us.

On Nov. 22, 1991, the movie was released to rapturous reviews. The grosses were record-breaking, the Oscar recognition extraordinary (see story on page 80). Today the film remains a high-water mark of the now virtually vanished world of hand-drawn animation—and a template for the continuing strength of animated musical films. Last September Lincoln Center held a 25th-anniversary screening, capped by Angela Lansbury—a few weeks short of her 91st birthday—appearing to sing the title song.

ANGELA LANSBURY
Thank God I've been able to continue to sing even at my advanced age. I wasn't out to prove anything. I just was out to remind the audience of the real person behind Mrs. Potts. Little children all over the world have recognized my voice for years. If they hear me in a store, they will often say, "Oh, that's Mrs. Potts!"

DON HAHN
When I look back at *Beauty and the Beast* now, what strikes me is how young and innocent most of us who made it were. The directors were in their 20s, as was much of the crew. Leaving a legacy was the furthest thing from our minds. We were just trying to revive animation and entertain the audience. We wanted a crack at putting our film out there with the greats we admired when we were growing up. We didn't know we couldn't do something like that. So we did.

▲ "Be Our Guest," sung by Jerry Orbach.

▶ Lansbury performs "Beauty and the Beast" at a packed screening for the film's 25th anniversary in New York.

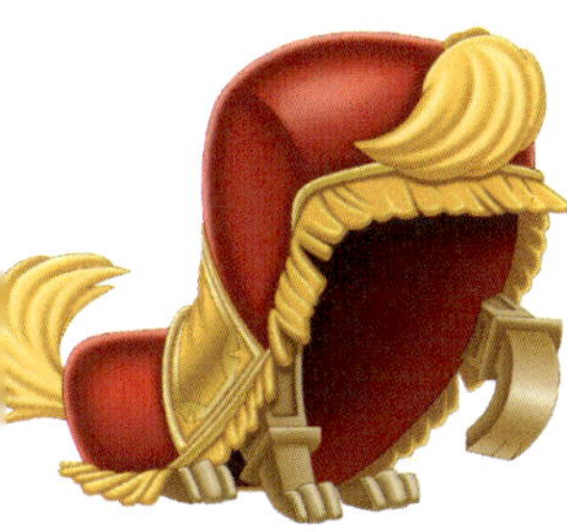

> On a demo, they sang [the title ballad] in a **ROCK STYLE.** I said, 'Look, if I may, I'd like to do a good Cockney sound for Mrs. Potts'"
>
> —ANGELA LANSBURY

Tales Behind the Tunes

After they took us under the sea with *The Little Mermaid*, composer Alan Menken and lyricist Howard Ashman returned to Disney to bring some musical-theater flair to *Beauty and the Beast*. Menken walks us through how the songs came to be. –BY DEVAN COGGAN

"BELLE"

The first song in the movie is the first one Menken and Ashman wrote. With dialogue sprinkled between the verses, this operetta-style prologue establishes the provincial French setting and introduces the bibliophilic heroine Belle (Paige O'Hara), who longs to escape its bounds. Its length and multitude of singing characters was unusual for a cartoon musical, which made Ashman nervous. "Howard was very reluctant to have us send it on to Disney," Menken says. "Basically he was saying, 'Who asked us for a seven-minute opening number? This is crazy. What are we thinking?' " But in the end, Disney execs were thrilled—and more than happy to say "bonjour" to "Belle."

"THE MOB SONG"

The final number is perhaps the darkest moment in the entire film, as Gaston (Richard White) leads the frantic villagers to the Beast's castle with torches and pitchforks. It's a grim theatrical sequence that Menken describes as "pure operetta." "In general," he says, "the tone of *Beauty and the Beast*, like *Little Mermaid*, was designed to capture the musical equivalent of the early Walt Disney movies, which were very European, very classic."

"SOMETHING THERE"

By the time Paige O'Hara and Robby Benson recorded the love song "Something There," Ashman had almost entirely lost his voice to complications from AIDS, but that didn't stop him from perfecting every musical moment. When O'Hara kept singing a sweet, slightly dreamy version of the line "New and a bit alarming," Ashman whispered a message to Menken: *Tell Paige on that line: Streisand.* "And she got it," Menken says. "'New and a bit a-LAR-ming.' That's exactly the performance she gave, and it gave exactly the sense of irony on that line."

"BEAUTY AND THE BEAST"

Menken and Ashman wrote two versions: a lullaby-like ballad for Angela Lansbury (with a demo by Ashman) and a poppier take for the radio (with a demo by Menken). But when Disney sent Lansbury the demo and invited her to play Mrs. Potts, she passed, saying the film didn't feel like a good fit. "What occurred to me was, 'That doesn't make sense. We literally wrote it for her,'" Menken recalls. "And I said, 'Well, which demo did you play for her?' 'Well, we sent her yours.' I said, 'Oh, no no no no no. Please, quick, send her Howard's!' I remember the sense of urgency!" After she heard the right demo, Lansbury immediately signed on—and recorded "Tale as Old as Time" in a single take.

"BE OUR GUEST"

Beauty and the Beast's biggest number started as a placeholder. When it came time to write the showstopper sung by Jerry Orbach, Angela Lansbury and the household staff chorus, Menken told Ashman, "'Okay, I'll give you a dumb piece of music that we'll throw out.' It was, to my mind, the most predictable, simple piece of music I could ever give him," he recalls. But once Ashman returned with lyrics, Menken realized he couldn't get that initial melody out of his head: "I simply could not improve upon that thing I had just thrown at him."

"GASTON"

The man who musically boasts "I use antlers in all of my decorating!" got a number that's part drinking song, part Sigmund Romberg waltz. Menken compares Ashman's swaggering "Gaston" words to those he wrote for the sadistic dentist in *Little Shop of Horrors*. "When that ['Gaston'] lyric was in front of me, I was just cracking up," Menken says. "It was so funny I could not get through it." Apparently no one makes Oscar-winning composers laugh like Gaston.

Tech Triumph

Ballroom Blitz

How an enchanting scene broke new visual ground and helped kick-start a golden age of CG wizardry. –**BY STEVE DALY**

FROM VIRTUAL-REALITY GAMING HEADSETS to superhero movies, photo-realistic computer-generated imagery—better known by the acronyms CGI and, more commonly, just plain CG, for computer graphics—has become omnipresent. We take it for granted these days that just about anything imaginable can be turned into convincing images.

But at the start of the 1990s, as *Beauty and the Beast* ramped up for production, the technology to produce elaborate CG was in its infancy. The most sophisticated computer systems at the time had maybe a tenth of the calculation and storage power you'd find in a smartphone today. That meant that filmmakers had to concentrate their resources on something manageable, like, say, a single CG character featured in an otherwise live-action movie, shown only in a limited number of shots.

James Cameron used this strategy to create the shape-shifting killer cyborg in 1991's *Terminator 2: Judgment Day.* But even as *T2* opened to enormous ticket sales over its July Fourth opening weekend, the *Beast* filmmakers were racing toward a November 1991 release-date deadline, unsure about a daring innovation of their own. For the now-indelible ballroom scene—wherein Belle and Beast waltz together and realize they're falling in love—the goal was to place hand-drawn animated characters believably in a three-dimensional, computer-rendered environment. The virtual camera would swoop and glide through the room and past a chandelier, dancing around the characters as they danced with each other. In live action, a crane shot would get the job done. Could the same be accomplished in animation, where flat background paintings had previously made it impossible to fully simulate movement through a space? Would the CG look incongruous in an overall 2-D, hand-drawn film, jolting the audience out of the romantic vibe instead of pulling it in?

"There was skepticism about it," recalls codirector Gary Trousdale. "It was experimental and fancy. We didn't know it was going to work." Earlier tests using CG to build an entire forest for the sequence where Belle fights off vicious wolves had taken months. When that footage came in, says Trousdale, "it was a disaster. We had to cut it and use conventional 2-D animation." In the wake of this misfire, nobody was looking to revive early talk of using CG in the movie's finale, where Gaston chases the Beast across castle rooftops in a driving rain. For the big production number "Be Our Guest," only a few fleeting shots of plates and glasses and a chandelier with dancing forks were used, gussied up with fast-moving hand-drawn accents and shown sparingly. But for the ballroom scene, the filmmakers hoped, maybe the existing technology would work more robustly. At the time, CG tools were already pretty good at rendering the sort of flat, smooth surfaces and geometrically regular windows and columns the space presented. All CG resources were shifted to the ballroom sequence, with fingers crossed.

While the tech team's first attempts at choreographing the action came off like a theme-park thrill ride—too many diving camera swoops plotted too aggressively—a revised version came together so well that even today it stands up, with no hint visible onscreen of the tension and effort that went into it. "It was one of those moments

The animation team originally designed a circular ballroom but switched to an oval (as seen in the film, left, and in a digital rendering, below), which allowed the filmmakers to use more interesting camera angles as they tracked Belle and the Beast's romantic waltz.

> "It drew **AUDIBLE GASPS** from the audience. It's the **PIVOTAL** point of the entire movie"
>
> —KIRK WISE, *codirector*

where the elements just all worked," recalls codirector Kirk Wise. "The expressiveness of the acting that animator James Baxter brought to both characters, the simplicity of the song itself, the freedom the camera had to move. At the time, it drew audible gasps from the audience. It's the pivotal point of the entire movie. And it's the sequence everybody remembers."

The ballroom scene electrified moviegoers and galvanized filmmakers. Both parties instinctively recognized a powerful new set of tools at work, even if the paying public—and plenty of studio executives—didn't quite understand all the details. Within a few years conventional hand-drawn animation wound up under siege as the dominant production format. Concurrently, so-called "practical" effects involving physical models became a tiny niche specialty. Hollywood would give us CG dinosaurs in *Jurassic Park* (1993), Jim Carrey as a human cartoon in *The Mask* (1994) and a room full of sentient plastic playthings in Pixar's 1995 debut CG feature, *Toy Story* (1995). Ticket sales zoomed, and studios followed the money.

As complex as CG visuals have grown in the years since, *Beauty*'s ballroom scene remains a model marriage of emotion and technology, content and form. Who doesn't long to linger in that elegant room? We're part of the action, laughing and pointing and oohing and aahing along with the cherubs in the ceiling painting at the sight of true love in its first delicate bloom—even as Beast's rose withers offscreen. It's visual storytelling at its finest, and three-dimensional in every way.

Disney Shakes Up the Oscars

The Academy rarely took animation seriously. But all that changed when *Beauty and the Beast* entered the picture.
—BY SHIRLEY LI

AS THE FIRST FULL-LENGTH ANIMATED FEATURE nominated for Best Picture, *Beauty and the Beast* had reason to celebrate even before it arrived at the 1992 Oscar ceremony. The decision to put a cartoon in the mix with *JFK* and *Bugsy* had been controversial. (And host Billy Crystal couldn't help but joke that Fievel, the mouse from *An American Tail,* hadn't received the news well, and "took an eraser to his wrists.")

But *Beauty* had a pride of place throughout the telecast. While it didn't take the top prize (that went to *Silence of the Lambs*), the film did earn two statuettes, for Original Song and Original Score. Audiences saw a cartoon Belle and Beast present the Best Animated Short trophy; a team of dancers interpreted the score; and members of the cast performed its three nominated songs.

The live crowd proved nerve-racking for the actors. Paige O'Hara, the voice of Belle, remembers standing backstage with Angela Lansbury before Lansbury performed "Beauty and the Beast" with Céline Dion and Peabo Bryson. "I could see Angela was really nervous too," O'Hara, recalls. "She said, 'When you get to my age, you learn when you're supposed to be nervous. This is it.' Then she took her hand and patted me on my bottom and said, 'But if I sang like you, I wouldn't be nervous.'" A jubilant rendition of "Be Our Guest" by Jerry Orbach followed.

But the evening had its share of somber notes as well. When Howard Ashman and Alan Menken won for the film's title song, Menken brought Ashman's longtime love, Bill Lauch, onstage to pay tribute to his late collaborator. And accepting Best Score, Menken said in his speech: "Howard, I wish you could have seen the finished product. I wish you could have heard the completed score. I know you would have been proud."

Certainly Ashman would have also been proud of the film's legacy with the Academy. It paved the way for the creation of the Best Animated Feature category in 2001 and opened doors for films like *Up* and *Toy Story 3* to receive Best Picture nominations down the line. "It was that feeling of 'Wow, Cinderella really did make it to the ball!'" producer Don Hahn told *Entertainment Weekly* in 2012, 20 years after the ceremony. "It was a chance to say, 'We really did a very cool thing with this movie and maybe changed the course of animation a little bit.'"

Jerry Orbach, who voiced Lumière, performing "Be Our Guest" with dancers at the 1992 Oscars.

Alan Menken holding his Best Original Song Oscar with Bill Lauch, the late Howard Ashman's partner.

▲
Orbach and dancers in the "Be Our Guest" number.

▶
Angela Lansbury during her performance of the Best Original Song winner, "Beauty and the Beast."

> "I could see Angela was really nervous too. **SHE SAID,** 'When you get to be my age, **YOU LEARN** when you're supposed to be nervous. **THIS IS IT**' "
>
> —PAIGE O'HARA

The Reanimation of Disney

In the late '80s, animated films at the studio of Mickey Mouse were all but dead. *Beauty and the Beast* helped further a renaissance that flourished well into the 1990s.
—BY PATRICK PACHECO

IN THE FALL OF 1991, DISNEY STUDIOS MADE one of the riskiest decisions in its history. The fabled company that Walt built decided to unveil an unfinished version of *Beauty and the Beast,* its new animated musical, at the New York Film Festival.

The elite audience of press and sophisticated moviegoers was at first mystified by the movie's inclusion in the festival. "We were all on pins and needles...sitting there holding our breath, because we didn't know what kind of reaction there would be," said Dick Cook, a Disney marketing executive at the time. "And when the movie finished, there was a pause...and all of a sudden the place just erupted." The sustained standing ovation was echoed in the rave reviews that followed when *Beauty and the Beast* hit theaters two months later.

Such glory could scarcely have been imaginable seven years earlier, when Disney's once-mighty animation department was in danger of being shut down. But it ended up undergoing a remarkable rebirth, a story recounted in the 2009 documentary *Waking Sleeping Beauty* (which—full disclosure—I wrote). It is a story of executives with no rules leading a passionately committed group of artists who would realize the full potential of the animated form with *Beauty and the Beast.*

Signs of new life emerged in the late 1980s, with the success of *Oliver & Company, Who Framed Roger Rabbit* and especially *The Little Mermaid.* The latter even won Oscars for the songwriting team Howard Ashman and Alan Menken.

The renaissance could never have happened without Roy E. Disney, Walt's nephew and vice chairman of the company, who'd warded off a shutdown of the animation department by bringing in the team of Michael Eisner and Jeffrey Katzenberg to lead the organization.

It was Katzenberg's friend, producer David Geffen, who'd suggested that Disney recruit Ashman and Menken, with whom he'd worked on the Off-Broadway hit *Little Shop of Horrors.* Coincidentally Peter Schneider, the young gun who was named vice president of feature animation, had worked as company manager on the same show.

Schneider, Ashman and Menken, along with Thomas Schumacher, a later hire, were steeped in the syntax and structure of the stage musical—songs that advanced plot and deepened character—and they tutored the Disney animators in that sensibility. Ashman, in particular, was acknowledged as the creative force behind the fledgling animation comeback. "There was real genius at work, and people knew it," said Katzenberg.

The concern that the success of *The Little Mermaid* might have been a fluke was compounded after an attempt to create a nonmusical version of *Beauty and the Beast* foundered. "After about six months we took the first 20 minutes of the film to screen for Jeffrey," recalled producer Don Hahn. "It

▲

Beauty and the Beast (far left) was released two years after *The Little Mermaid* (above), a smash hit that saved Disney's animation department from extinction.

◀

Pixar's *Toy Story*, the first feature-length computer-generated animated movie, put an exclamation point on Disney's extraordinary return to form—and changed the industry forever.

wasn't perfect, but what was the worst that could happen? They weren't going to scrap it and start all over again. That would be just insane." Katzenberg scrapped it and told them to start all over again. Hahn rebounded by tapping two relatively neophyte directors, Kirk Wise and Gary Trousdale, and by persuading Ashman and Menken to postpone their passion project *Aladdin* and join the *Beauty* team.

The initial domestic ticket sales of more than $150 million for *Beauty and the Beast* signaled that Disney's animated musicals were no longer relegated to the kiddie table. The lines outside the theaters were peopled with young adults—a stunning turnaround, since just years earlier a survey had revealed that the majority of teens wouldn't be caught dead at a Disney animated feature.

While *Beauty and the Beast* would lose the Best Picture Oscar, the honors, box office success and lucrative merchandising served to shift Disney's focus away from live action to animation. That move would be more than justified with its next film, 1992's *Aladdin*. Heated up by Robin Williams's manic turn as the genie and Ashman, Menken and Tim Rice's memorable songs, the film bettered its predecessor by grossing $504 million around the world.

The phenomenal one-two punch drew the attention of other movie studios, which rushed to develop their own animation departments. At Disney, animation artists were transformed from a group of people wondering if their careers were dead to rock-star-like industry leaders with sizable bonuses, lucrative competing offers and frequent television appearances.

These were heady times. The artists campaigned feverishly to become a part of *Pocahontas*, since it was touted as being the Next Big Thing at the studio, while another project in development, a coming-of-age tale about a lion cub, was dismissed as a chancy experiment. As it turned out, *Pocahontas* topped out at $141 million in North America and $346 million worldwide, while *The Lion King* grossed $422 million domestically and just under a billion dollars worldwide. Later, spiked by the global success of its stage version, *The Lion King* would become one of the most successful entertainment enterprises in history.

The triumph of *Beauty and the Beast* lured back to the studio such Disney alumni as Tim Burton, who produced *The Nightmare Before Christmas* in 1993. And when Schneider could not persuade John Lasseter to leave Pixar to join the Disney team, the exec arranged a joint venture and three-picture deal, which yielded a little buddy comedy called *Toy Story*, the first feature-length computer-generated movie and the beginning of an industry-changing franchise.

In the 25 years since *Beauty and the Beast* was released, animation has continued to flourish. In 1991 *Beauty* was just one of a handful of releases. Last year alone there were more than two dozen qualifying for the Best Animated Feature Oscar that was instituted in 2001.

Most of those were computer-generated. So it's striking to remember that parts of the unfinished *Beauty and the Beast* film that so enraptured the New York Film Festival audience were black-and-white, hand-drawn sketches. The simple lines—hearkening back to a tradition that had given birth to *Pinocchio, Sleeping Beauty, Bambi* and other classics—would not only transform a beast into a prince but revitalize a studio and revolutionize an entire industry.

> Animation artists were transformed from **A GROUP OF PEOPLE** wondering if their **CAREERS WERE DEAD** to rock-star-like industry leaders

▲ Robin Williams voiced the genie in 1992's *Aladdin*, a massive worldwide hit.

► Beginning with the 1994 movie, *The Lion King* became one of the most successful entertainment franchises of all time.

Fairy Tale in the Flesh

In 1994 *Beauty and the Beast* became Disney's first Broadway smash, opening the stage door for *The Lion King, Aladdin* and a new era in American musicals.

BY ISABELLA BIEDENHARN

IT'S HARD TO IMAGINE BROADWAY TODAY without Disney's thumbprint all over it—but before 1991, adapting a cartoon for the stage was virtually unheard of. "It's pretty simple: No one thought about it," says Thomas Schumacher, president and producer of Disney Theatrical Group. "At the time the focus was [either] go to see a movie or come to one of our theme parks." There was also a financial concern: Why would the Walt Disney Corporation sink millions of dollars into a stage production that might not pay out for at least a year—if it was successful—when it could open an animated film on a Friday and make its money back by Sunday?

That year, however, two crucial elements converged at just the right time. Robert Jess Roth, the 27-year-old who would eventually become director of *Beauty and the Beast* on Broadway, had been staging live productions in the studio's various venues and finally persuaded Disney's CEO, Michael Eisner, and chairman, Jeffrey Katzenberg, to let him attempt a

Toni Braxton (center) joined the Broadway cast as Belle in 1998. Alan Menken and Tim Rice wrote a new song for her, "A Change in Me," which became a permanent addition.

Broadway adaptation of *Mary Poppins.* Shortly afterward, in November 1991, *Beauty and the Beast*—the studio's masterpiece—was released in theaters to a chorus of enthusiastic reviews.

Roth and his creative partners saw the film the night it opened. "We were blown away by it," he remembers. "[It had] the most beautiful artwork, the most amazing score from Alan Menken and Howard Ashman." It was also naturally suited to the stage because, as Roth notes, Ashman, Menken and screenwriter Linda Woolverton had actually "set out to do a Broadway show as an animated musical."

Two days after the film's release, bolstered by its positive reception, Eisner suggested that Roth and his team shelve *Mary Poppins* and work on adapting *Beauty* instead. One major challenge presented itself immediately: How do you ask an actor to play...a teapot? "We came up with this idea to change the mythology of the movie a little bit," Roth says. In the film the enchantress's spell turns everyone in the castle into objects instantly. "We said, 'What if the spell is that he's slowly changing into a beast as the petals fall off the rose, and all the inhabitants of the castle are slowly changing from human beings into objects?'" he says. "Then you're not asking an actor to be a teapot. You're asking them to be a person with an affliction."

Disney brass approved the tweak, and after Roth and his team presented their full vision, the board of directors authorized a reported $12 million budget. Seven songs were added to the show—six brand-new ones from Menken writing with Andrew Lloyd Weber's frequent lyricist Tim Rice and one Menken-Ashman number, "Human Again," that had been cut from the film. An eighth arrived in 1998: When Toni Braxton joined the cast as Belle, Menken and Rice wrote a song called "A Change in Me" just for her—and it was such a hit that it remains in the stage production to this day.

Beauty and the Beast completed a 1993 tryout run in Houston before opening on Broadway on April 18, 1994, at the Palace

▲ Andrea McArdle as Belle in a 1999 performance of *Beauty and the Beast* in New York City.

► Donny Osmond played Gaston on Broadway in 2006.

> “What if the spell is that he’s **SLOWLY CHANGING** into a beast as the petals fall off the rose, and all the inhabitants of the castle are slowly changing from **HUMAN BEINGS TO OBJECTS?**”
>
> —ROBERT JESS ROTH, *director of the musical*

A FROZEN TREAT

THE BEAST ON BLADES

In 1996 Disney's long tradition of adapting its properties to the rink welcomed Belle and the Beast into its on-ice gang. —BY ISABELLA BIEDENHARN

Viktor Petrenko and Ekaterina Gordeeva appeared in the 1996 television special *Beauty and the Beast: A Concert on Ice.*

Disney has been in the ice business since 1981—long before it released *Frozen*—staging big-budget Disney on Ice shows with sensational special effects. Put on through Feld Entertainment, the same company that owns the Ringling Bros. and Barnum & Bailey Circus, the shows have long been a treat for tykes who could travel (and whose parents could afford tickets). But in 1996 Disney's *Beauty and the Beast: A Concert on Ice* television special brought the magic straight into kids' homes. Broadway stars Susan Egan and James Barbour hosted the program and performed the show's musical numbers, while Olympic figure skaters Ekaterina Gordeeva (Belle) and Viktor Petrenko (the Beast) acted out an adaptation of the story—complete with sophisticated set pieces on the rink itself. The special went on to earn three Primetime Emmy nominations in 1997, winning a statue for Outstanding Technical Direction. Offscreen Belle and the Beast have continued to skate into children's hearts on Disney on Ice's tours alongside other beloved characters, from Mickey Mouse to Buzz Lightyear.

Theatre. The original Broadway cast included Susan Egan as Belle, Terrence Mann as the Beast, Burke Moses as Gaston, Gary Beach as Lumière and Beth Fowler as Mrs. Potts. Like its source material, the show was a smash with audiences (though critics' enthusiasm didn't reach quite as high), and it took mere days for other countries to pursue their own productions. In 1994 *Beauty and the Beast* was nominated for nine Tony Awards, though its only win went to costume designer Ann Hould-Ward.

A multigenerational appeal is one clear reason for the musical's success. "*Beauty and the Beast* had this distinction of simultaneously being a family show and a date-night show, and that's a unique thing," Schumacher says. "The show would have died if it were just for kids." Tickets also became more exclusive—and pricier—after the production moved from the Palace to the smaller Lunt-Fontanne Theatre in 1999.

The show's statistics are breathtaking: *Beauty and the Beast* ran on Broadway from April 18, 1994, to July 29, 2007, for 5,461 performances and grossed $429,158,458. It's currently the 10th-longest-running production in Broadway history and has been translated into nine languages and performed on every continent but Antarctica for a total of 35 million people.

And, as a piece of live theater, *Beauty and the Beast* is still very much living and breathing. Roth recalls working on the most recent American tour, in which the actors playing Belle and Gaston asked to modify the scene where he walks her home. "They wanted to play it like he was a fly and she was shooing him away... like he's a little bit annoying, but he's not threatening," Roth says. "It was a lighter touch that was really clever, and it gave us somewhere bigger to go—because by the end of the show, *he's* the beast."

The tale may be as old as time, but it can always be freshened up. As Schumacher says, "*Beauty and the Beast* is now a classic in the catalog of musical theater. Just like opera and classical music live on... this show will long outlive us."

▲ Hugh Jackman as Gaston (top left), with castmates Cindy Pritchard, Alinta Carroll, Mark Dickinson, Laura Hamilton and Grant Smith in a 1995 Melbourne production.

▶ Susan Egan as Belle and Tom Bosley as her papa, Maurice, in 1994. Both were members of the original Broadway cast.

> “*Beauty and the Beast* had this **DISTINCTION** of simultaneously being a **FAMILY SHOW AND A DATE-NIGHT SHOW**, and that's unique”
>
> —THOMAS SCHUMACHER, *Beauty's theatrical producer*

CASTING A WIDE NET

BELLES OF THE BALL

Hundreds of actresses have played the heroine who tames the Beast. Here are six of them, starting with the OG herself, Susan Egan. —BY ISABELLA BIEDENHARN

Susan Egan
(Broadway 1994, Los Angeles 1995-96)

Kerry Butler
(Broadway 1996-97)

Deborah Gibson
(Broadway 1997-98)

Toni Braxton
(Broadway 1998-99)

Andrea McArdle
(Broadway 1999-2000)

Jamie-Lynn Sigler
(Broadway 2002-03)

The Stage Show by the Numbers

24

HOURS IT TOOK TIM RICE TO WRITE A COMPLETELY NEW SONG FOR TONI BRAXTON

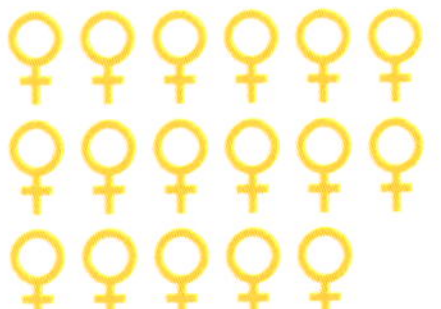

17

WOMEN WHO HAVE PLAYED BELLE ON BROADWAY

35

MILLION PEOPLE ON PLANET EARTH WHO HAVE SEEN *BEAUTY AND THE BEAST* THE MUSICAL

115

CITIES AROUND THE WORLD THAT HAVE HOSTED PRODUCTIONS OF THE SHOW

$429,158,458

LIFETIME BROADWAY BOX OFFICE **GROSS**

40+

POUNDS WEIGHT OF BELLE'S BALL GOWN

32,000

TIMES GASTON PUNCHED LEFOU ONSTAGE BY THE END OF THE BROADWAY RUN

TONY NOMINATIONS THE SHOW RECEIVED IN 1994

400

HOURS OF HUMAN LABOR PUT IN TO CREATE THE FIRST BEAST COSTUME

(which used 20 pounds of human hair!)

11

MAGIC TRICKS IN THE SHOW, DESIGNED BY JIM STEINMEYER & JOHN GAUGHAN

(illusionists who've worked with David Copperfield and Siegfried & Roy)

BY ISABELLA BIEDENHARN

$1,481,663: TOTAL SUM RAISED BY THE PRODUCTIONS FOR BROADWAY

$1.4 BILLION

TOTAL WORLDWIDE BOX OFFICE **GROSS** OF ALL VERSIONS OF THE STAGE SHOW

3

TIMES *(in a row)* DIRECTOR ROBERT JESS ROTH WATCHED *BEAUTY AND THE BEAST* AT LONG BEACH'S AMC MARINA PACIFICA 6 CINEMA IN 1991

120 WIGS

WORN ONSTAGE EVERY NIGHT, IN EVERY VERSION THROUGHOUT THE WORLD

CARES/EQUITY FIGHTS AIDS

ENTERTAINMENT WEEKLY
Editorial Director Jess Cagle
Editor Henry Goldblatt
Creative Director Tim Leong
Executive Projects Director Erik Forrest Jackson

BEAUTY AND THE BEAST
Editor Missy Schwartz
Editor, People + EW Books Allison Adato
Designer Sung Choi
Photo Editor Robert Conway
Writers Isabella Biedenharn, Devan Coggan, Clark Collis, Steve Daly, Shirley Li, Patrick Pacheco, Alyssa Smith
Reporters Blake Bakkila, Daniel S. Levy
Copy Desk Joanann Scali (Chief), James Bradley (Deputy), Ellen Adamson, Gabrielle Danchick, Matt Weingarden (Copy Editors)
Production Designer Joni Danaher
Premedia Executive Director Richard Prue
Senior Manager Romeo Cifelli
Manager Rob Roszkowski
Imaging Production Associate Franklin Abreu, Ana Kaljaj
Research Director Céline Wojtala

TIME INC. BOOKS
Publisher Margot Schupf
Associate Publisher Allison Devlin
Vice President, Finance Terri Lombardi
Vice President, Marketing Jeremy Biloon
Executive Director, Marketing Services Carol Pittard
Director, Brand Marketing Jean Kennedy
Sales Director Christi Crowley
Assistant General Counsel Andrew Goldberg
Assistant Director, Production Susan Chodakiewicz
Senior Manager, Category Marketing Bryan Christian
Brand Manager Katherine Barnet
Associate Project Manager & Production Anna Riego
Associate Prepress Manager Alex Voznesenskiy

Editorial Director Kostya Kennedy
Creative Director Gary Stewart
Director of Photography Christina Lieberman
Editorial Operations Director Jamie Roth Major
Senior Editor Alyssa Smith
Associate Art Director Allie Adams
Assistant Art Director Anne-Michelle Gallero
Copy Chief Rina Bander
Assistant Managing Editor Gina Scauzillo
Assistant Editor Courtney Mifsud

SPECIAL THANKS
Brad Beatson, Melissa Frankenberry, Kristina Jutzi, Simon Keeble, Seniqua Koger, Kate Roncinske, Kristen Zwicker

Published by Time Inc. Books
225 Liberty Street
New York, NY 10281

We welcome your comments and suggestions about Entertainment Weekly Books. Please write to us at: Entertainment Weekly Books, Attention: Book Editors, P.O. Box 62310, Tampa, FL 33662-2310
If you would like to order any of our hardcover Collector's Edition books, please call us at 800-327-6388, Monday through Friday, 7 a.m.–9 p.m. Central Time.

PHOTO CREDITS
COVER Disney; **BACK COVER** Disney; **Pg 1:** Laurie Sparham/Disney; **Pg 2-3:** Laurie Sparham/Disney; **Pg 4-5:** 1991 poster: Disney/Photofest; 2017 poster: Disney; Condon, Watson: Laurie Sparham/Disney; **Pg 6-7:** Love Me Tonight: Alamy; Condon, Watson: Laurie Sparham/Disney; **Pg 8-9:** Disney; **Pg 10-11:** Laurie Sparham/Disney; **Pg 12-13:** (clockwise) Laurie Sparham/Disney (2); Disney; **Pg 14-15:** (clockwise) Laurie Sparham/Disney (2); Disney; Laurie Sparham/Disney; **Pg 16-17** Disney (2); **Pg 18-19:** Laurie Sparham/Disney (2); **Pg 20-21:** (top) Laurie Sparham/Disney (2); (bottom) Disney (2); **Pg 22-29:** Laurie Sparham/Disney (7); **Pg 30-32:** Kerry Hallihan (2); **Pg 33:** Laurie Sparham/Disney; **Pg 34-35:** Snow White: RKO Radio Pictures/Photofest; Cinderella: Disney; Sleeping Beauty: Disney/Photofest; The Little Mermaid: Disney; Beauty and the Beast: Disney; **Pg 36-37:** Aladdin: Buena Vista Pictures/Photofest; Pocahontas: Disney; Mulan: Disney/Everett Collection; The Princess and the Frog: Disney; Brave: Pixar/Disney; Frozen: Disney; Moana: Disney; **Pg 38-39:** Marais: Sunset Boulevard/Getty Images; Stevens as the Beast: Disney; Stevens: JB Lacroix/WireImage; sketch: Disney; **Pg. 40-41:** Cadenza and Tucci: Disney (2); Kline and Gad, Evans: Laurie Sparham/Disney (2); **Pg 42-43:** Disney (7); **Pg 44:** Disney/Photofest; **Pg 45:** Carolyn Cole/LA Times/Contour by Getty Images; **Pg 46-47:** Laurie Sparham/Disney; **Pg 49:** Garderobe and Ashman: Disney (2); McKellan: Olivier Vigerie/Getty Images; **Pg 50-55:** Disney (10); **Pg 56-57:** Disney; **Pg 58-59:** Belle at window: Laurie Sparham/Disney; Disney (2); **Pg 60-61:** Disney (3); **Pg 62-63:** Disney; **pg 64-65:** 1537: Erich Lessing/Art Resource, NY; 1946: Sunset Boulevard/Getty Images; 1962: United Artists/Photofest; 1984: Koch Vision; 1987 film: Cannon Films/Everett Collection; 1987 TV: CBS Photo Archive/Getty Images; 1991: Disney; 2011: Takashi Seida/CBS Films; 2014: Capital Pictures; **Pg 66-67:** Stiers, Lansbury, Orbach: Disney/Photofest; enchanted objects: Disney; animator Mark Henn: Disney/Everett Collection; **Pg 68-69:** Disney (4); **Pg 70-71:** Disney (4); **Pg 72-73:** sketch: Disney; Lansbury and family: MPTV; Belle, Maurice: Collection Christophel/Disney/Alamy; Cogsworth,Lumiere: Disney; **Pg 74-75:** Lansbury: Kristina Bumphrey/StarPix/REX/Shutterstock; Disney (3); **Pg 76-77:** The Mob Song: Disney/Entertainment Pictures/Zuma Press; Disney (5); **Pg 78-79:** Belle and Beast: Disney/Alamy; rendering: Disney; **Pg 80-82:** Copyright©Academy of Motion Picture Arts and Sciences (3); **Pg 83:** MPTV; **Pg 84-85:** Belle: Disney; The Little Mermaid: Buena Vista Pictures/Photofest; Toy Story: Pixar/Disney; **Pg 86-87:** Disney (2); **Pg 88-89:** Joan Marcus; **Pg 90-91:** McArdle: Joan Marcus; Osmond: Donna Ward/Getty Images; Concert on Ice: Everett Collection; **Pg 92-93:** Jackman and cast: Karen Dodd/Newspix; Sigler: John Barrett/Globe Photos/Zuma; Joan Marcus (6); **Pg 94-95:** globe: Ingram Publishing/Getty Images; Belle: Joan Marcus; Tony: Tony Cenicola/The NY Times/Redux; wig: Frazer Harrison/Getty Images; **Pg 96:** Disney

THE ROSE
For the bloom that sheds petals as long as the Prince fails to earn true love, production designer Sarah Greenwood and set director Katie Spencer supervised the creation of several handcrafted hybrids that married real roses and leaves on artificial stems.

THE CLOCHE
Made by Swarovski, the bell jars used during production were etched by a London engraver. Its French rococo design intentionally mimics the frost engulfing the Prince's castle.

THE TABLE
To fit into the castle's design, the art department also created this bespoke baroque table, the top of which was made from a special black-and-gold marble called cosmic.

Printed in Great Britain
by Amazon